60268A

S0-AXK-470

FORDHAM
UNIVERSITY
AT
TARRYTOWN
LIBRARY

FORD
UNIV
AT
TARRYTO

GARLAND STUDIES ON THE ELDERLY IN AMERICA

edited by

STUART BRUCHEY
UNIVERSITY OF MAINE

A GARLAND SERIES

THE INNER-CITY ELDERLY

How Effective Are Their Support Structures?

ROBERT N. DeLEAIRE

FORDHAM
UNIVERSITY
AT
TARRYTOWN
LIBRARY

GARLAND PUBLISHING, Inc.
New York & London / 1994

Copyright © 1994 Robert N. DeLeaire
All rights reserved

Library of Congress Cataloging-in-Publication Data

DeLeaire, Robert N. (Robert Nathaniel), 1935–
    The inner-city elderly : how effective are their support structures? /
Robert N. DeLeaire.
        p.   cm. — (Garland studies on the elderly in America)
    Includes bibliographical references and index.
    ISBN 0–8153–1703–4 (alk. paper)
    1. Poor aged—New York (N.Y.)—Social conditions.   2. Minority
aged—New York (N.Y.)—Social conditions.   3. Aged—Services for—
New York (N.Y.).   I. Title. II. Series.
HQ1064.U6N457   1994
305.26'09747'1—dc20   94–10895
                                                              CIP

FORDHAM
UNIVERSITY
AT
TARRYTOWN
LIBRARY

Printed on acid-free, 250-year-life paper
Manufactured in the United States of America

Contents

List of Tables.. vii

Preface xi

Introduction xiii

Chapter

  I.   Social Characteristics of the Elderly:
      The United States and the *Easyride* Sample.......... 3

      The Nationwide Situation 3

      The Urban Situation... 5

      Summary and Forecasts 15

  II.   Social Supports: The Family............................... 17

      The Minority Family... 20

      I. Family Support.. 23

      II. Relative-Kinship Support........................... 38

      Summary.. 40

  III.   The Role of Physical Health 43

      Summary.. 52

  IV.   Social Agency Utilization 55

      The Senior Centers.. 57

The Role of the Church................................... 62

Summary... 66

V.   Life Satisfaction: Morale, Well-Being,
      and Life Expectations 69

Life Satisfaction in Relation to
the Environment... 70

Life Satisfaction and Fear of Crime................ 73

Composite Measure of Life Satisfaction.......... 76

Summary... 86

VI.   Summary and Conclusions 87

Afterword.. 91

Appendix... 93

Statistical Procedures..................................... 93

Composite Indices.. 95

Selected Bibliography 99

Index.. 113

Tables

1.1 Interviews Completed And Completion Rates: Public Housing For The Elderly 6

1.2 Location Of Subjects 8

1.3 Ethnicity (By Project) 8

1.4 Age Distribution 9

1.5 Ethnicity (By Age Range) 9

1.6 Marital Status 10

1.7 Ethnicity (By Marital Status) 11

1.8 Marital Classification (By Sex) 12

1.9a Financial Resources (By Ethnicity and Pension Benefits) 13

1.9b Financial Resources (By Ethnicity and Social Security Benefits) 13

1.10a Income Adequacy (By Ethnicity) 14

1.10b Income Adequacy (By Age) 15

2.1 With Whom Do You Live (By Ethnicity) 24

2.2a Living Children (By Gender of Respondent) 25

2.2b Number of Living Children (By Age of Respondent) 25

2.2c Number of Living Children (By Ethnicity of Respondent) 26

2.3a   Frequency of Seeing Children
       (Respondents Age 65–71)...................................... 27

2.3b   Frequency Of Seeing Children
       (Respondents Age 72–76)...................................... 27

2.3c   Frequency Of Seeing Children
       (Respondents Age 77–80)...................................... 28

2.3d   Frequency Of Seeing Children
       (Respondents Age 81+) 28

2.4   Frequency of Seeing Children
       (By Marital Status and Ethnicity) 29

2.5   Frequency of Seeing Children
       (By Ethnicity and Marital Status) 30

2.6   Frequency of Seeing Children
       (By Ethnicity and Gender)..................................... 31

2.7   In Some Emergency, Can You Depend on
       Children, Their Spouses, Or Close Friends To
       Help You? (By Ethnicity)...................................... 32

2.8   If You Need Help For a Longer Period,
       Can You Depend On Your Children, Their
       Spouses, Or A Close Friend To Help You?
       (By Ethnicity).. 33

2.9a   Where Does Your Child Live? (By Ethnicity and
       Age: Respondents Age 65–71) 34

2.9b   Where Does Your Child Live? (By Ethnicity and
       Age: Respondents Age 72–76) 34

2.9c   Where Does Your Child Live? (By Ethnicity and
       Age: Respondents Age 77–80) 35

2.9d   Where Does Your Child Live? (By Ethnicity and
       Age: Respondents Age 81+)................................. 35

2.10a Where Does Your Child Live? (By Ethnicity
       and Gender: Men) 36

2.10b Where Does Your Child Live? (By Ethnicity
       and Gender: Women).. 36

2.11   If Some Emergency Came Up In The Lives
       Of Your Children, (Or Close Friend), Is It Likely
       That You Would Go and Help Out?
       (By Ethnicity).. 37

2.12a Frequency Of Seeing And Visiting Relatives
       (By Gender) 38

2.12b Frequency Of Seeing And Visiting Relatives
       (By Age)... 39

2.12c Frequency Of Seeing And Visiting Relatives
       (By Ethnicity).. 40

3.1   Self-Evaluation Of Health (By Ethnicity
       and Gender).. 45

3.2   Self-Reported Health Status (By Ethnicity
       and Age)... 46

3.3   Self-Reported Health Status (By Ethnicity
       and Marital Status)... 48

3.4a   Frequency Of Doctor Visitation (By Ethnicity)... 49

3.4b   Frequency Of Doctor Visitation (By Gender, All
       Groups Combined).. 50

3.4c   Frequency Of Doctor Visitation (By Age)........... 50

3.5   Frequency of Doctor Visits (By Marital
       Status, All Groups Combined).............................. 51

4.1   Frequency Of Going To Governmental
       Agencies.. 56

4.2   Frequency Of Going To The Senior Center......... 58

4.3   Frequency Of Going To The Senior Center
       for Lunch (By Age)... 59

4.4   Satisfaction With The Senior Center
       (By Gender) 60

4.5   Frequency Of Going To The Senior Center
        For Lunch (By Cohabitation)............................... 61

4.6   Frequency Of Going To The Senior Center
        For Lunch (By Ethnicity)...................................... 62

4.7a   Frequency of Church Attendance (By Gender) ... 63

4.7b   Frequency of Church Attendance (By Age) 64

4.7c   Frequency of Church Attendance
        (By Ethnicity)... 65

5.1   Satisfaction With Housing (By Ethnicity)........... 71

5.2   Satisfaction With Neighborhood (By Ethnicity).. 72

5.3a   Fear Of Being Mugged During The Day
        (By Ethnicity)... 74

5.3b   Fear Of Being Mugged During The Day
        (By Gender) 75

5.4   Distribution Of Factor Scale Loadings 77

5.5a   Composite Index Of "Trust"
        (By Ethnicity and Marital Status) 78

5.5b   Composite Index of "Trust"
        (By Ethnicity and Gender)................................... 79

5.5c   Composite Index of "Trust"
        (By Ethnicity and Age).. 80

5.6a   Composite Index of "Optimism"
        (By Ethnicity and Marital Status) 81

5.6b   Composite Index of "Optimism"
        (By Ethnicity and Gender)................................... 83

5.6c   Composite Index of "Optimism"
        (By Ethnicity and Age).. 84

5.7   Composite Index of "Anxiety" (By Ethnicity
        and Marital Status)... 85

Preface

Aging is one of a series of developmental phases of the life span. It is not a static phenomenon which comes at the end of the organism's existence, but rather a fluid state influenced by one's physiology, psychology, and their economies, and the socio-economic and cultural environment in which it lives and whose attitudes the organism embraces, applies to itself and reacts to accordingly.

To be sure, one out of one ages, yet it is the above-mentioned variables, which, to my mind, bring the aging process at varying rates and in a varying way to different individuals regardless of their chronological years. Each phase in the individual's development, in its quest for adequate adaptation, has some aspects which are common to all, yet each phase also has some problems which are unique to it and it alone.

J. Weinberg
"Personal and Social Adjustment in Aging," pp. 17–20, in J. F. Anderson (ed.), *Psychological Aspects of Aging*. Washington, D.C.: American Psychological Association.

Introduction

This work reports an inquiry into the conditions of life of low-income elderly residents of New York City. Specifically, it is concerned with the urban Black and Hispanic elderly, and examines their social supports, health, and life satisfactions. Both of these minority populations are heavily dependent on public resources for their housing, transportation, and physical and mental health needs.

Presently, there are over twenty million individuals who have passed their sixty-fifth birthday and millions more in the pre-retirement cohort between 55 and 65 (1980). The number of Americans 65 years and over is more than six times as great today as it was in 1900.

This figure is expected to rise significantly in the near future as breakthroughs are made in controlling diseases that afflict the aged. It is estimated that by the year 2000 there will be more than 28 million people who are over 65. It is further estimated that the population composed of the very old (over 75) will increase at about twice the rate of the over-65 group as a whole, and at more than twice the rate of the total population.

In a special study made by the Bureau of the Census in 1975, women accounted for 109.14 million, or 51.3 percent, of the United States' population. This means the number of women in this country exceeds that of men by 5.6 million. Moreover, projections for 1985 and 2000 show the disparity will increase to between approximately 6.2 and 6.5 million.

Even as the proportion of the United States population that is old increases, the elderly population itself will become older. At present 9.1 percent of those in the 65-and-over age group are aged 85 and above. This percentage will grow steadily to 16.7 in 2010, then drop back to lower levels until after 2030, as the baby boom attains age 65 but not age 85. Afterwards it would climb again to where one-quarter of the elderly in 2080 will be over age 85. To one extent or another, this phenomenon occurs because of projected increases in life expectancy (United States Department of Commerce, Bureau of the Census, 1985).

The twentieth century has seen a dramatic increase in the number of aged Blacks and Hispanics in the United States (Lambing, 1972). Between 1900 and 1967, life expectancy at birth increased by 28.6 years for Black males to 61.1 years, and by 35.0 for Black females to 68.2 years. Their White counterparts showed gains of only 19.6 and 24.0 years. Thus, the problems of aging will increasingly affect members of the Black community.

Profile of Inner-City Elderly

In presenting a profile of the New York City inner-city elderly, Cantor (1973) reports:

First, the inner-city elderly comprise nearly 30 percent of the city's present population of persons 60 and over. It is within these areas that large and growing concentrations of Black and Hispanic elderly are found, which indicates that the inner city has increasingly become the home of the city's minorities. Nonetheless, the majority of elderly in these areas are still White.

Second, ethnicity has a considerable effect on age distribution. If we consider old age as having a beginning, middle, and ending periods, we find that the Hispanic elderly are clustered in the initial period — they are the youngest of the elderly, with two-thirds under 70. The Black elderly tend to be somewhat older than the Hispanic but younger than the Whites. Nearly 60 percent of the

Blacks are under 70, as compared with only half of the White elderly.

Several cultural factors apparently contribute to these age differences. The most important is differential longevity. Black life expectancy is seven years less than that of Whites, and, although exact data with respect to mainland Puerto Ricans are lacking, it is believed that a similar differential exists for them. Another factor that has contributed to ethnic differences in age distribution in the city is the tendency for Blacks and Puerto Ricans to return "home" upon reaching old age. However, this out-migration factor is expected to fade to lesser importance with respect to succeeding generations of Blacks and Spanish elderly.

Marital Status

In reference to marital status, more Hispanic elderly have been married and, in part because they are the "youngest" elderly, more are presently married — 43 percent are living with a spouse. The White elderly are the next most likely to still be married — 30 percent. Although the Black elderly had the second highest rate of marriage, at this point in their lives they are the least likely of the three sub-groups to be still married — 29 percent. It is the Black respondents who report the highest rate of separation or divorce. Among the White elderly population is found the largest number of persons who have never married at all. This leads us to the question of the possibly special role of single males and females among the aged.

Gender

In trying to understand the situation of older women within the urban setting, our discussion would be remiss if we did not include the developing roles of older minority women. Hispanic and Black women together represent over 40 percent of New York City's female population (Cabrera, 1978). According to the 1980 Census, approximately

951,932 New Yorkers are 65 and older. Fifty-nine percent, or six out of every ten, are women. Of this population, more than half (57 percent) are widowed, separated, or divorced, as compared to only 22 percent of the men. More significant, perhaps, is the fact that 45 percent, or nearly half, of all older women live alone, as compared to 35 percent of all adult women.

Before pursuing this, though, it is important to bring out a few facts about older women. Brophy (1978) informs us that in 1976 there were 12.7 million women 65 years of age and over, with 573,000 or 4.5 percent of them living in New York City. Nationally, 53 percent of these women were widowed, and 40 percent were living alone. Marital status is a major difference between older men and older women. While 76 percent of men 65 and older are married, only 36 percent of women in this group are married. Men who are widowed are socially sanctioned both to pursue a new spouse and to marry women younger than themselves. The older woman, however, is put into the double bind of not being as free as her male counterpart to find a new spouse, and also of losing much of her identity and economic status when her husband dies. The reported median income in 1975 for men over 65 years was $4,959, while for women it was $2,642. The problem of insufficient income is the major problem they face.

A crucial fact of life for many of the elderly is that old age is synonymous with poverty. This was borne out in the 1980 census, which informed us that half of all families headed by persons 65 and over had incomes of less than $12,295 per year, less than half the median income attained by younger families. With regard to the median income for the nearly one million elderly persons in New York City, about two out of five had incomes of less than $5,000 per year, and half of these had incomes of less than $3,000 a year. About 5 million older Americans fall below the poverty level. Moreover, elderly people form a growing proportion of those living in the inner city. The aged poor have been unable to join younger, more affluent citizens in their flight to the suburbs, and hence concentrate in inner cities that have deteriorated. The inner city will thus become more and more the home of the aged poor.

Among America's elderly population, the inner-city poor unquestionably encounter the greatest financial and personal hardships. A VERA Institute of Justice study (1978) disclosed a number of carefully defined problems that generally plague the elderly poor: transportation, meals, medical care, visiting with friends and family, quality of housing, adequate employment opportunities, provision for voluntary tasks, and psychological dispositions (i.e., the correlates of "life satisfaction").

If there is any group of the aged that requires special assistance, it is found in the inner city where financial circumstances force Blacks, Hispanics, and Whites into impoverished integrated neighborhoods. This research will analyze this economically deprived segment of the elderly. What we will learn from this may determine what social policy measures, if any, can be implemented to improve their circumstances.

Gelwicks *et al.* (1971) inform us that the residential environment can be either a facilitator or a constraint on the individual in his or her pursuit of daily activities. By providing access to needed services, the environment can have important and direct influences on daily activity patterns, mobility, and social interaction, as well as indirect effects on health and well-being.

Neighborhood

Analyses of the development and functions of cities have brought to our attention that cities are primarily social organizations (Birren, 1969). When we are young, we are flexible, mobile, and adaptable to the structures of the city. However, as we age, our physical and psychological strengths wane. Consequently, our ability to make movements and changes to different locations is greatly reduced. The aged, therefore, become more dependent upon resources within the immediate community to meet their needs. Researchers and census information have informed us that the elderly of the inner city are essentially long-term residents of the areas in which they live (Cantor, 1973). Virtually all have lived in their neighborhoods at least 10 years or more, and over half have 20 or more years of residency in the same neighborhood. It is clear that their roots are deep and that they are familiar with their neighborhoods and how to negotiate their way around. However, as they cease to work, grow older and frail, and their incomes become more limited, they are increasingly neighborhood-based and neighborhood-bound.

Health

As we increase in age, there are both increasing health problems and decreasing energies which affect the quality of our lives. If income is the number one problem of older people, health care is a close second. To define "health," I accept Stanley Brody's definition, which describes it as "the ability to function well physically and mentally and to express the full range of one's potentialities" (1973).

Concern about health and illness has been cited most frequently as a cause of worry by the elderly living in the inner city (Cantor and Mayer, 1974). Most of the respondents in their study perceive themselves in good health, have a relatively low rate of hospitalization, and continue to perform the tasks of daily living with little or no difficulty. But concern about health is always with them, and the adequate delivery of health services is essential not only for their current health status, but as a means of preventing future institutionalization.

Historically, medicine has been concerned with the understanding and management of disease (Richmond, 1969). Preventive efforts have been based primarily on disease prevention rather than health maintenance and optimum functioning. The medical system has been concerned with the quantity rather than quality of life. However, there are other socio-psychological factors which strongly influence the state of a person's health and functioning. These include not only the general environment but the many protective sub-systems such as the family and, more broadly, the public-private organizations of health care delivery. Thus, people's index of health and their ability to rally from insults depend not only on their own capabilities but also on the supports necessary and available to enable them to achieve optimum functioning.

Poor health is not distributed evenly among the elderly population in the inner city. Factors such as age, sex, ethnicity, living arrangements, and above all, income, appear to have an effect on health status. Hispanic and Black elderly perceive their health as substantially less favorable than do their White peers. Thus, only 20 percent of the Whites feel they are in poor health, while among the Hispanic elderly 31 percent feel that they are in poor health, and only 23 percent of the Black elderly find their health good. Researchers, namely Cantor *et al.*, have noted the tendency of Spanish-speaking populations, particularly the women, to verbalize illness more readily. This may be due to cultural differences in terms of the acceptability of ill health. Given the lower standard of living experienced by most Black and Hispanic elderly during their formative childhood and adult years, it is likely that the reported differential in health status among the three subgroups of respondents is an accurate reflection of physiological reality.

Studies have indicated that more than half of the elderly in the inner city were rated as having some impairment, ranging from mild disability to incapacitation. In studying the three subgroups that make up the New York inner-city population, the Hispanics (who reported the poorest health) were similarly rated the most impaired.

Contrary to the differences in self reports of health status, there appears to be no measurable difference between Blacks and Whites in the level of impairment. Elderly women in the inner city reported having higher levels of incapacity than did men, probably due to the fact that persons living independently in their own homes ("live-alones") were significantly more likely to have some impairment in functional ability than were those who lived with a spouse. In a recent study of health conducted by Butler and Newacheck (1981), the authors reported that the 34 million Americans in the poorest families, those with incomes below $6,000 a year, average about twice as many days sick in bed or otherwise restricted in their normal routines as the rest of the population. Further, most of this health gap is due to greater levels of chronic illness, such as heart disease, arthritis, and hypertension, among the poor. Although government spending for social programs has more than doubled since the mid-1960s (after adjusting for inflation), government health policy has failed to recognize the severity of chronic illness among the poor.

In an urban-industrial-technological society, the support system of the aged increasingly involves an amalgam of services offered by large-scale organizations, whether they be governmental or voluntary. Presently, it is government that provides the floor of basic services for older people in such crucial areas as income maintenance (SSI), health (Medicare), and transportation (reduced fares). But it is the family and significant others who retain considerable importance, particularly in meeting the more personal needs of the individual.

Cantor (1974) suggests that most of the inner-city elderly have a primary support system made up of family and neighbors. However, eight percent of his sample of 80,000 older persons in the inner city appeared to have no inter-personal system and were entirely on their own. Some few of these were in touch with community or religious institutions, but the absence of any "close other" suggests that they are likely to be true isolates.

Environmental and Life Satisfaction

In *The Urban Elderly*, Berghorn *et al.* stress the fact that older people, along with other age groups, must operate within a given social and economic environment, and that for the most part, such environments are not created with the needs of older people in mind. However, when the environment includes convenient transportation, safe neighborhoods, and adequate health care facilities, the older person's life experiences are likely to be more satisfying. On the other hand, an environment that lacks such attributes decidedly limits a person's chances to achieve a satisfying life in his or her later years.

Transportation services, such as EASYRIDE, which provided the elderly disabled with van transportation to and from clinics, hospitals, and agency programs whether for the physically handicapped or for the aged, mean more than simply getting from one place to another. They are the link to all the other activities that make contact and participation in religious, social, and recreational activities possible. In addition, better access to medical care and to nutrition programs can have the consequence of improved health, better access to social life, improved feelings of self-worth, and better ability to handle one's daily affairs independently. Obviously, if the elderly and disabled can manage in their homes on their own or with some help, they will not need the constant care and supervision that is available only in institutions.

The degree to which services for the elderly and disabled can help avoid or defer institutionalization is an important question because not only do people by and large not want to live in institutions, but because institutional care is enormously expensive. The percentage of persons in long-term care is low — only 5 percent of those over 65 now live in long-term facilities. However, that percentage increases steeply in age groups over 75, and even a small percentage increase represents a large number of people and a very high cost. Therefore, to the extent that EASYRIDE helped to prevent or defer institutionalization, it performed a substantial service to both the individual and society.

Thus, the poorer health status of the inner-city elderly, including the high incidence of chronicity, is certainly indicative of the need for medical services, particularly in the case of older Hispanic and Black elderly, and those living alone. To what extent are the elderly receiving the attention they need?

The concepts of life satisfaction, morale, and adjustment have long played an important role in social gerontology (Cutler, 1980). In earlier research, they were often used as interchangeable labels for a general set of concerns. Similarly, measures of those concepts were typically used as dependent variables in efforts to trace the impact of specified life-course changes such as widowhood, retirement, residential changes, and decrements in health upon aging adults. While the range of variables that influence life satisfaction may be broad and numerous, the effects of two potentially significant variables on life satisfaction have remained relatively obscure. These, as reported by Donnerwerth *et al.* (1978), are residence (rural or urban) and race.

Some researchers have argued that urban residence, particularly in deteriorating neighborhoods, has a negative effect on life satisfaction or a sense of well-being (Lawton and Kleban, 1971; Lawton and Cohen, 1974). Edwards and Klemmach (1973) and Hynson (1975) found general happiness to increase as the size of the city of residence decreased. However, from an activity perspective, as noted by Philblad and McNamara (1965), it can be argued that the aged in rural areas experience greater isolation from relatives and friends and thus are likely to have lower life satisfaction. Bultena (1969) reported that the urban elderly have significantly more interaction with their children than do the rural elderly. This interesting finding calls for further interpretation, and some new insights regarding this situation and other correlates of life satisfaction will be offered in this study.

The EASYRIDE Study

In 1978, the VERA Institute of Justice conducted a research program that addressed some of the needs of aged citizens in an urban area. The aim of the study was to gather baseline and comparative data for the evaluation of

EASYRIDE, a transportation service designed for the special needs of the aged and disabled. The study did not, however, address specific issues affecting elderly Black and Hispanic persons, nor did it take into account the fact that the minority component of the aged and disabled population is growing steadily and is increasingly straining urban service delivery systems. It is under these constraints that the current study re-examines the VERA Institute data in an attempt to ascertain if it is feasible to develop new social programs and policies to serve the urban minority aged.

The major objective of the VERA (EASYRIDE) study was to implement a comprehensive low-cost door-to-door/demand-response transportation system so as to increase the mobility of those who are handicapped and can use the public transportation system only with difficulty or not at all. More specifically, the program attempted to demonstrate that EASYRIDE would allow its passengers to make more trips out of the house, or to make them with less difficulty and stress, and in ways that better satisfy their needs.

This research will analyze:

1. Social support networks (emotional well-being, self-esteem, and networking).

2. Health (self-perceived diagnosed chronic conditions, and professionally evaluated conditions as measured by health providers).

3. Life satisfaction (autonomy, competence, morale).

In line with these broad considerations, this study will focus on several specific objectives. These include:

• Describing the social and physical condition of the elderly poor.

- Assessing their self-perceived needs and the services provided them.

- Comparing different ethnic low-income aged groups, namely, Blacks, Hispanics, and Whites, and paying special attention to elderly women.

The study will also focus on the role of ethnicity in the relationship between the etiology of conditions and the adjustments made to these conditions.

Summary

Identifying the extent to which the inner-city neighborhoods of New York offer the elderly proximity to vital goods and services in order to enhance their mobility, social-support interaction, and life satisfactions is the objective of this research.

As outlined, this study will provide a more conclusive analysis of the situation of the urban minority elderly. The examination will focus upon the significance of social environments (neighborhoods), social supports (both formal and informal), self-perceived health status, and the degree of life satisfaction.

The Inner-City
Elderly

Social Characteristics of the Elderly:
The United States and the *Easyride* Sample

The Nationwide Situation

A nationwide demographic profile of older Americans in the 1980 Census reported that our nation's population has 25.5 million persons aged 65 years and older. Of these 25.5 million persons, there are 15.2 million women and 10.3 million men, or 148 older women for every 100 older men. The ratio of women to men increases with age, ranging from 125 for the 65–69 group to a high of 229 women to 100 men for persons 85 and older. Of the over-65 population in 1980, 15.6 million were between 65 and 74 years of age, 7.7 million were 75–84 years old, and 2.2 million were 85 years old or older. In 1980, persons reaching age 65 had an average expectancy of an additional 16.4 years. Women at 65 could expect to live an additional 18.4 years; men could expect an additional 14.1 years.

Locations

People 65 and older were slightly less likely to live in metropolitan areas than were younger persons (64% of the elderly and 68% of other ages). The elderly are less likely to change residence than members of other age groups. Of those who did move, the majority moved to another home in the same state, although a significant number had moved from the Northeast or North Central regions to the South or West.

Racial and Ethnic Composition

In 1980, not quite 90% of persons 65 and over were White, 8% were Black, 3% were of Hispanic origin, and about 2% belonged to other races.

Living Arrangements

The majority (68%) of older non-institutionalized persons lived in a family setting in 1980. Approximately 8.1 million (83%) older men and 8 million (57%) older women lived in families. The proportion living in a family setting decreases with age. Nearly one-third (7.1 million) of all non-institutionalized older persons lived alone. This included 41% of older women and 15% of older men (5.7 million women, 1.4 million men). An additional two percent of both men and women, or one-half million older persons, lived with non-relatives.

Marital Status

In 1980, almost twice as many older men were married as older women (78% of older men and 40% of older women). However, there were more than five times as many widows (7.1 million) as widowers (1.3 million). Slightly more than half of the older women were widows (51%).

Income

Families with a 65 year old or older head of household had a median income in 1980 of $12,882 ($13,382 for Whites and $8,363 for Blacks). One out of every five (21%) families with an elderly head of household had incomes of less than $7,500 in 1980. Conversely, 18% of such families had incomes of $25,000 or more.

Elderly persons living alone or with non-relatives were likely to have low incomes, with 60% receiving $6,000 or less per year. Nearly one-third (32%) of them had incomes under $4,000 a year, while only 18% received $10,000 or

more. The median income for these individuals was $5,096
($5,354 for Whites and $3,718 for Blacks).

Poverty

The poverty rate for persons 65 and over was almost
16% in 1980, higher than the 13% for the general
population. Another 2.5 million, 10% of the elderly, were
classified as "near-poor" (income between the poverty level
and 125% of poverty). In total, one-fourth of the older
population was poor or near-poor in 1980.

One out of every seven (14%) elderly Whites was poor,
as were more than one-third (38%) of the elderly Blacks and
nearly one-third (31%) of the elderly Hispanics.

More elderly living alone or with non-relatives were poor
(31%) than were elderly living in families (9%). The
proportion of elderly living below the poverty level was
higher in non-urban areas (21%) than in urban areas (13%).

The Urban Situation

The Lower East Side of New York City has appeared so
often in the literature of those seeking their American roots
that it is almost mythical to many of us. But it is a real place,
a two square-mile area of lower Manhattan Island, where in
the 19th and early 20th centuries waves of immigrants settled
and took root.

Traditionally, the Lower East Side has been bounded on
the west and east by the Bowery and the East River, and on
the north and south by Houston Street and the Brooklyn
Bridge. When the areas was chosen in 1976 by the VERA
Institute for its pilot project in transportation (EASYRIDE)
for the elderly and handicapped, the traditional Lower East
Side area was expanded to include Little Italy, Chinatown,
and the East Village as well. From this location, generations
of the vigorous and successful have risen out of the Lower
East Side to prosperity and even fame. Those who have been
left behind, plus the less successful newcomers to the area

(escaping even less tolerable situations elsewhere) make up the population served by EASYRIDE. These are the people living out their lives in a geographic area emotionally meaningful to them, even though their situations are not ideal. Many live alone, many live with part-time government subsidized companions or helpers, and many others live with equally enfeebled spouses (A. Simmel *et al.*, 1978).

The table which follows gives the target sample sizes and the completion rates achieved in the face-to-face interviews for the surveys that were completed.

Table 1.1

Interviews Completed And Completion Rates:
Public Housing For The Elderly

	Target Sample	Number of Interviews	Percent Completed
Lower East Side	466	332	71
Bronx and Chelsea	252	193	77
Total	718	525	73

This target sample was made up of new EASYRIDE registrants who had registered with the service in May and June of 1978. The initial aim of the sampling procedure was twofold:

• to obtain samples from the general population of older or disabled people; and

• to obtain significant numbers of respondents having particular handicaps.

The assumption was that handicapped people would not be included in sufficient numbers in any random sample of the general population. The samples of the residents of public housing for the elderly were intended to be a particular part of the general population — not a representative sample, but a part distinguishable in terms of demographic and economic characteristics from the general population of older people in the Lower East Side, Chelsea, and the Bronx. The relatively high number of non-respondents for this study includes a relatively high ratio of refusals. There was no good explanation for this high rate of refusal. Some evidence suggests that heavier users of EASYRIDE were more likely to have many health problems. It is not an unreasonable speculation that health problems play a role in refusal rates.

The total number of elderly covered by the study consisted of 525 persons: 424 of these were age 65 and older. The 101 others were either relatives and/or severely handicapped persons, and thus eligible for the EASYRIDE pilot program. All subjects lived in government-sponsored housing or low-cost housing within the boroughs of New York. The subjects resided in locations shown in Table 1.2 on the following page.

Within this population there were 119 men and 296 women, or a grand total of 415 persons. Four persons were not reported, and five members of the EASYRIDE population were Asian, and are not included in this analysis.

Table 1.2

Location Of Subjects

House	Number of Persons
The Bernard Baruch Houses 72 Columbia Street	63
The Fiorello LaGuardia Houses 282 Cherry Street	87
The Meltzer Houses 94 East 1st Street	110
The Chelsea Houses 430 West 26th Street	56
The Bronx River Houses East 174th Street	108
Total	N = 424

An analysis of ethnicity by project reveals the following distributions:

Table 1.3

Ethnicity
(By Project)

House	Black	White	Hispanic
Bernard Baruch	3	29	29
La Guardia	12	63	11
Meltzer	3	90	17
Chelsea	8	28	19
Manor Drive	29	30	14
Bronx River	13	17	4
Subtotals		257	94
Total N = 419			

In terms of age, the sample can be divided into four meaningful groups:

Table 1.4

Age Distribution

Age Range	Number	Percentage
65–71 (Young Old)	103	24
72–76 (Middle-Aged Old)	111	26
77–80 (Older-Aged Old)	104	25
81–96 (Frail old)	106	25
Total	N = 424	100

The respondents were classified by these age categories in order to make better use of the age variables in this analysis. These four age groups vary considerably in terms of ethnicity, with Hispanics the youngest and Whites the oldest.

Table 1.5

Ethnicity
(By Age Range)

Age Range	Blacks		Whites		Hispanics	
	#	%	#	%	#	%
65–71	18	26	49	19	36	38
72–76	18	26	60	23	33	35
77–80	18	26	71	28	15	16
81–96	14	21	77	30	10	11
Subtotals	68	99	257	100	94	100

Total N = 419

Missing observations = 5

In terms of marital status, the respondents are distributed as follows:

Table 1.6

Marital Status

Classification	Number	Percent
Never Married	53	13
Married	101	24
Widowed	224	53
Divorced	22	5
Separated	21	5
No Answer	3	< 1
Total	424	100

This chart clearly demonstrates the predominance in our sample of widowed persons. Those who live with a spouse and those who now live alone for reasons other than widowhood are equal in numbers, with each category making up about one quarter of the sample.

In analyzing marital status by ethnic category, we see the following:

Table 1.7

Ethnicity
(By Marital Status)

Marital Status	Blacks		Whites		Hispanics	
	#	%	#	%	#	%
Never Married	5	7	38	15	9	10
Married	11	16	64	25	24	26
Widowed	43	63	141	55	39	42
Divorced	2	3	11	4	9	10
Separated	7	10	2	1	11	12
Subtotals	68	99	256	100	92	100

Total N = 416

Missing observations = 3

Finally, in examining marital status by sex, we see the following distribution:

Table 1.8

Marital Classification
(By Sex)

Classification	Men		Women	
	#	%	#	%
Never Married	24	20	28	10
Married	47	40	53	18
Widowed	31	26	187	64
Divorced	8	7	14	5
Separated	8	7	12	4
Subtotal	118	100	294	412
% of Total	29%		71%	

Missing observations = 12

Table 1.8 supports the gerontological literature that women do outlive their spouses. Consequently, they must prepare themselves for the situation of being alone in their senior years. (Even though there are more married elderly women than married elderly men in terms of number, this does not apply by percent.) By and large, males have a shorter life span.

In examining the socioeconomic status of this population, the data inform us that almost all of these persons are retirees and that they derive their income either from pensions or Social Security benefits. Within this population of respondents, 99% (418) were classified as Not Employed. One respondent was employed full-time and three respondents were employed part-time.)

Table 1.9

Financial Resources

(a) By Ethnicity and Pension Benefits

Pension	Black		White		Hispanic	
	#	%	#	%	#	%
Union Pen.	62	91	213	83	82	88
Employee Pen.	5	7	36	14	9	10
Veteran's Pen.	1	2	8	3	2	2
Subtotals	68	100	257	100	93	100

Total N = 418

(b) By Ethnicity and Social Security Benefits

Pension	Black		White		Hispanic	
	#	%	#	%	#	%
Social Security	29	43	174	68	43	46
SSI	5	7	12	5	21	22
Old Age Asst.	34	50	68	26	29	31
Non-recipients	—	—	3	1	1	1
Subtotals	68	100	257	100	94	100

Total N = 419

The data in Tables 1.9a and 1.9b indicate that these respondents subsist primarily on governmental and non-governmental financial programs. Four hundred (95%) respondents reported that they have no savings accounts, while twenty-one (5%) respondents reported that they are living partially on money withdrawn from their savings accounts.

Table 1.10a

Income Adequacy
(By Ethnicity)

Adequacy	Blacks		Whites		Hispanics	
	#	%	#	%	#	%
Cannot make ends meet	15	22	29	11	14	15
Just enough, no more	46	69	210	82	71	77
Enough, a little extra sometimes	6	9	13	5	6	7
Always have money left over	0	0	4	2	1	1
Subtotals	67	100	256	100	92	100

Total N = 415

Missing observations = 4

Table 1.10a suggests that the incomes of most respondents are marginally adequate, although Blacks and Hispanics are more likely to report that their incomes are inadequate.

Table 1.10b

Income Adequacy
(By Age)

Adequacy	65–71		72–76		77–80		81+	
	#	%	#	%	#	%	#	%
Cannot make ends meet	13	13	14	13	18	17	13	12
Just enough, no more	75	74	89	81	80	78	88	83
Enough, a little extra sometimes	12	12	6	5	5	5	2	2
Always have money left over	1	1	1	1	0	0	3	3
Subtotals	101	100	110	100	103	100	106	100

Total N = 420

Table 1.10b indicates that age per se apparently makes no important difference in reports of income adequacy, although the "young old" may have a slight edge in terms of receiving more than a necessary minimum.

In essence, this older population (EASYRIDE) is a low income group. Shelter and health costs must be paid first. The remainder means minimal expenditures for "necessities" such as food and clothing and even smaller expenditures on such "luxuries" as transportation and recreation.

Summary and Forecasts

In summary, I have presented a profile and demographic description of the low-income inner-city elderly who are in a quasi-independent status. They are self-sufficient in many areas, yet they are dependent upon many governmental services. In the following chapters, I shall examine this inner-city elderly population by looking at their relationships to their family, kin, and supportive social networks; their physical health status, their use of agencies; and finally, their levels of life-satisfaction.

By so doing, we will see if this urban inner-city elderly population differs from the nationwide elderly.

Social Supports: The Family

In urban industrial society, the support system of the elderly increasingly involves an amalgam of informal services provided by family, friends, and neighbors, and formal services offered by large organizations, both governmental and voluntary. The emphasis in this section of the study will be on the family, particularly children, and the extent and types of relationships which exist between older people and their kin.

There is ample evidence that adult children continue to provide help to their parents (Shanas, 1979, 1980; Sussman, 1965). However, there are many trends in modern society that act to limit the extent to which adult children are willing or able to provide help to their elderly parents (Treas, 1977; Ward, 1978). Since the adult children are both an essential and a limited support system for elderly parents, it is most important to understand the factors that elicit and sustain their helping behavior.

Social support can be defined as the belief, or the experiences on which the belief is based, that one is cared about, loved and esteemed, and that one belongs to a network of communication and mutual obligation that can be activated in time of need. Since the family is usually considered the quintessential source of social support, questions were asked as to the frequency of contact with them, and whether they can be relied upon to help out in emergencies or for longer periods of time. In addition, since friends can also be important sources of social support, questions were asked about respondents' contacts with them.

Sussman (1965) found that the extensiveness of help to elderly parents and the length of time it is offered depend on the extent of the mutual aid and socialization patterns already in existence. Somewhat in the same vein, Bengston, Orlander, and Haddad (1976) proposed a model of intergenerational solidarity in which helping behavior was seen as an aspect of intergenerational solidarity in that helping behavior itself was seen as a function of the dependency needs of the elderly, residential propinquity, filial responsibility, and sex linkage. According to such a model, there would be more helping behavior when the parent's dependency needs became greater, when the adult child lived closer, and when the adult child was a daughter. Various studies have made it clear that, in the context of care giving to the elderly, the word "family" most often means the women in the family (Lang and Brody, 1983). Elderly wives (helped by daughters) are the caregivers for ailing or disabled husbands, while adult daughters (and to a lesser extent, daughters-in-law) usually have the responsibility for widowed older people (Shanas, 1979; Sussman, 1965; Townsend, 1968; Tobin and Rulys, 1980). Much current thinking in the field derives from this and other comparable sociological research.

The psychological tradition can also be of value in explaining the long-lasting dyadic bond between parent and child and the motivations toward helping behavior that stem from that bond. The theory of attachment, although originating in the study of the infant-mother relationship, has much to offer when applied to the relationship later in life.

Cicirelli (1983) maintains that "attachment refers to an emotional or affectional bond between two people; essentially it is based on being identified with, in love with, and having the desire to be with another person. As such, it represents an internal state within the individual, which can be inferred from a stable propensity over time to seek proximity and contact with the attachment figure, even though actual proximity seeking behavior may appear only occasionally or be absent for extended periods."

Troll, Miller, and Atchley (1979) have developed a path-analysis of supportive help activities across generations which they have outlined as follows:

A. Help flowing downward from the old to the young;

B. Help flowing from the middle generation both upward to their parents and downward to their children; and

C. Help flowing reciprocally among all generations.

Therefore, patterns of help during the family's life cycle shift in response to the changing needs and capacities of family members.

According to Bowlby (1979), attachment to a parent does not end in childhood or early adolescence, but endures throughout the life span along with the related attachment, exploratory, and protective behavioral systems. In extending the idea of attachment throughout the life span, the authors (Troll and Smith, 1976; Hartup and Lempers, 1973) are concerned with the unilateral attachment of the child to the parent — not only with the reciprocal relationship between parent and child, but new multiple attachments that the individual develops, such as friends, objects, or other family members.

Attachment behavior in adulthood has been defined by Cicirelli (1983) as a class of behaviors including the interaction of communication over distance to maintain psychological closeness and contact, in addition to periodic returns to the parent to re-establish physical closeness and contact. Examples of such attachment behaviors are residential proximity to the parent; periodic visits; and communication through telephoning, letter writing, and messages sent through others.

Protective behavior in adulthood is exemplified in adult children's caregiving behaviors to their elderly parents. When the attachment bond is threatened by the parent's illness or deprivation, the adult child who is attached will provide care to maintain the survival of the elderly parent and preserve the emotional bond.

Cicirelli (1983) further maintains that if one conceives of attachment between child and parent as being related to reciprocal helping behavior, with the balance of help shifting from being in favor of the child in the earlier portions of the life span to being in favor of the parent in the later part of the life span, then one can think not only in terms of species survival through survival of the young but also of the fulfillment of the elderly's potential life span before death. Subsequently, attachment behaviors are regarded as preceding protective (or helping) behaviors, for some contact and communication must take place before the need for help can be ascertained and the actual helping can occur.

The Minority Family

In examining the family structures and the mutual support systems that aid the elderly within minority families, researchers have found that the situation within black families is different from that within white families. Because of this difference, the minority elderly have a different set of salient group structures as available choices. The family structures that are available to the minority elderly are the products of a historical process that has placed them in a relatively disadvantaged position. Within the black subculture, both the different systems of meaning and the social structures appear to be due to the historical and continuing state of minority group status (Mindel and Hayes, 1973). It has been pointed out by various researchers (Aurantelli, 1960; Drabeck and Boggs, 1968; Schelsky, 1954) that in times of crisis individuals tend to rely upon the family as a source of material, social, and emotional support. Adams (1970) has pointed out that minority status tends to strengthen kin ties because of the need for mutual aid and survival in a hostile environment.

Mindel and Hayes (op. cit.) hypothesized that:

A. Black families have more contact with their kin than do white families.

B. Black families have more extended kin living in the same household than do white families.

C. Black families receive more help from kin in child care and rearing than do white families.

D. Black families have more frequent contact with a wider variety of kin than do white families.

E. Black families perceive their extended kin as more significant than do white families.

In a study of "The Elderly in the Inner-City" by the New York City Department for the Aging (1973), ethnicity and socio-economic status were key variables utilized in an attempt to understand the life of New York's older residents. Cantor (1973) posed the following questions in her study:

1. Do Blacks and Spanish speaking elderly enter the period of old age with greater social, economic, and physical deficiencies than do their white elderly cohorts?

2. Do the living patterns of the Black and Hispanic communities, particularly the extended or augmented family structure and its attendant value system, tend to mitigate against role loss and social isolation?

Cantor found that many of the Spanish elderly (more than their Black or White peers) were still functioning within the protective environment of the extended family. As elders they tend to interact strongly with their children, both as advice givers and as assisters in a variety of tasks from babysitting to shopping to fixing things in their children's homes. With less money, they are not as apt to give children material gifts but appear to have outlets for giving of themselves and a role to play within the family circle. However, the problematic situation is that 27 percent of the Spanish elderly live alone, rather than within the extended family, and they show signs of mental stress and worry to a far greater degree than do the black or white elderly. Seemingly, they worry most about children and family matters.

As for the black elderly, Cantor found they are also facing many of the same economic and minority group problems as the Hispanic elderly, without some of the redeeming features of close-knit extended family life. A somewhat different family pattern emerged. Black parents help children out somewhat less often than Spanish elderly, but seem to play a more direct role in the functioning of their children's households than do the white elderly. They give gifts as freely as their white peers although they have less income, and in turn children are available for assistance in time of crisis. However, it was also reported that intervention on the part of the children on a day-to-day basis was not as frequent as among Spanish families.

In relation to the white elderly in the poverty areas, a conflicting picture was presented, in that most had been lower-middle or middle-middle class during their adult years and old age brought them not only role loss but severe economic and often social discontinuity. Although most had living children in the New York metropolitan area with whom they were in contact, or at least "felt close," in most cases generational separation went along with geographical distance. Children and parents helped each other in times of crisis, but involvement in the details of daily living was neither expected nor desired on the part of the white elderly, as many of their children lived beyond the immediate neighborhood. Love and affection was shown through gifts, money, visiting, telephoning and emergency help or occasionally baby-sitting, but other types of more direct intervention, including advice giving, were rare.

Gibson (1972) suggests the need to define and examine the following factors in family interaction: the availability of kin, the proximity of kin, the frequency of kin contact, and the functionality of kin. He notes that the availability of kin is of particular importance since the traditional measures of kin interaction (e.g., proximity, frequency of contacts, etc.) usually fail to take into account the pool of relatives or significant others who are actually available for interaction.

I. Family Support

One concern of this study is to determine the extent to which older people in the urban community receive meaningful support from those around them, since merely having a living child or friend, or simply knowing a neighbor, is not in and of itself enough.

The significant question is:

Is the older person's relationship with those around him or her ongoing and steady enough to provide meaningful social support?

The concept of *functionality* (Gibson *et al.*, 1972) will be utilized and defined in the following way:

A *functional spouse* is defined as one with whom one lives.

A *functional child* or *sibling* is someone whom the respondent sees at least monthly or is in telephone contact with at least weekly.

A *functional relative* is one living within the city area and who is seen or heard from regularly.

My analysis based on these definitions will serve to sharpen the concept of support network so that it will include only persons in a position to offer meaningful support to the elderly, both in times of crisis and on a continuing basis. Thus, this chapter will focus on the kinship network, and the impact of ethnicity on it.

Table 2.1

With Whom Do You Live?
(By Ethnicity)

	Blacks	Whites	Hispanics	Total
Live	79%	75%	74%	75%
Alone	(54)	(190)	(69)	(313)
With	16%	23%	24%	22%
spouse	(11)	(58)	(22)	(91)
Spouse in	—	1%	—	22%
institution	—	(2)	—	(2)
Relatives	4%	2%	2%	2%
or friends	(3)	(4)	(2)	(9)
Total	(68)	(254)	(93)	(415)
Percent	16.3%	61.4%	22.3%	100%

Missing observations = 7

Within our population of elderly, Table 2.1 demonstrates that among the three ethnic groups, three quarters of the respondents lived alone. There is no significant difference between the three ethnic groups in percentage of elderly living alone. We see also that Hispanics and Whites were slightly but not significantly more likely to have a living spouse, so that at a time of need or crisis they would have a person in the immediate household on whom they could rely. Blacks were less likely to be living with a spouse, possibly due to the shorter life expectancy of males.

At this point, it is important to examine our respondents to see how many have and do not have children. This information will provide us with a clearer idea of the makeup of their support systems. In so doing, we find that 68 percent (237) of this population have children and 32 percent (137) do not. By cross-tabulating by gender, marital status, age, and ethnicity, we were able to learn the following:

Table 2.2a

Living Children
(By Gender of Respondent)

	Male	Female	Total
With living children	57% (68)	72% (213)	68% (281)
Without living children	43% (51)	28% (83)	32% (134)
Total	(119)	(296)	(415)
Percent	29%	71%	100%

Missing observations = 9

Table 2.2b

Number Of Living Children
(By Age of Respondent)

	65–71	72–76	77–80	80+	Total
With living children	69% (71)	66% (73)	77% (80)	59% (63)	68% (287)
Without living children	31% (32)	34% (38)	23% (24)	41% (43)	32% (137)
Total	(103)	(111)	(104)	(106)	(424)
Percent	24%	26%	25%	25%	100%

Table 2.2c

Number Of Living Children
(By Ethnicity of Respondent)

	Black	White	Hispanic	Total
With living children	71% (48)	67% (171)	70% (66)	68% (285)
Without living children	29% (20)	33% (86)	30% (28)	32% (134)
Total	(68)	(257)	(94)	(419)
Percent	16%	61%	23%	100%

Missing observations = 5

With this information (from Tables 2.2a–c), we have learned that two-thirds of this population of elderly persons, without regard to age, gender, or ethnicity have adult children whom they can utilize as helping agents at time of need or crisis. Logically, the "never married" are the ones with the fewest living children who might be utilized for helping purposes. The question arises as to who might help them? How sustaining would the caregiver efforts be? For how long a period of time? These questions will be statistically examined and answered in the latter part of this chapter.

In further examining this possible support system, especially as it may involve adult children, respondents were asked about frequency of seeing their children. We excluded those persons who did not have children.

Table 2.3a

Frequency Of Seeing Children
(Respondents Age 65–71)

	Black	White	Hispanic	Total
At least once a week	53% (7)	32% (10)	7% (2)	27% (19)
A few times a month – twice a year	38% (5)	26% (8)	55% (15)	39% (28)
Once a year or less/never	7% (1)	42% (13)	36% (10)	34% (24)
Total	(13)	(31)	(27)	(71)
Percent	18%	44%	38%	100%

Table 2.3b

Frequency Of Seeing Children
(Respondents Age 72–76)

	Black	White	Hispanic	Total
At least once a week	33% (5)	32% (12)	38% (8)	34% (25)
A few times a month – twice a year	27% (4)	27% (10)	38% (8)	30% (22)
Once a year or less/never	40% (6)	40% (15)	24% (5)	36% (26)
Total	(15)	(37)	(21)	(73)
Percent	20%	51%	29%	100%

Table 2.3c

Frequency Of Seeing Children
(Respondents Age 77–80)

	Black	White	Hispanic	Total
At least once a week	31% (4)	23% (12)	38% (5)	27% (21)
A few times a month – twice a year	31% (4)	29% (15)	38% (5)	31% (24)
Once a year or less/never	38% (5)	48% (25)	23% (3)	42% (33)
Total	(13)	(52)	(13)	(78)
Percent	17%	67%	16%	100%

Table 2.3d

Frequency Of Seeing Children
(Respondents Age 81+)

	Black	White	Hispanic	Total
At least once a week	17% (1)	38% (19)	— —	33% (20)
A few times a month – twice a year	67% (4)	36% (18)	50% (2)	40% (24)
Once a year or less/never	17% (1)	26% (13)	50% (2)	27% (16)
Total	(6)	(50)	(4)	(60)
Percent	10%	83%	7%	100%

Table 2.4

Frequency Of Seeing Children
(By Marital Status and Ethnicity)

	Widowed			All Other		
	B	**W**	**H**	**B**	**W**	**H**
More than once a week	30% (10)	32% (35)	32% (9)	50% (7)	30% (17)	17% (6)
A few times a month – twice a year	30% (10)	36% (40)	39% (11)	50% (7)	19% (11)	51% (18)
Once a year or less	39% (13)	32% (35)	29% (8)	— —	51% (29)	31% (11)
Total	(33)	(110)	(28)	(14)	(57)	(35)

B = Black
W = White
H = Hispanic
Missing observations = 11

In inquiring as to how often the respondents had contact with their children either by telephone or by letter, the statistical responses were not significantly different. The majority (White) respondents had a slightly higher percentage of telephone or mail contacts than the minority (Black and Hispanic) respondents. Despite not being statistically significant, this finding tends to support the earlier reported observation that the Whites also continue to have numerous and frequent filial contacts, even though they are more geographically removed.

Table 2.5

Frequency Of Seeing Children
(By Ethnicity and Marital Status)

	Widowed			Not Married			Married		
	B	W	H	B	W	H	B	W	H
At least once a week	30% (10)	32% (35)	32% (9)	57% (4)	33% (3)	17% (3)	43% (3)	29% (14)	18% (3)
A few times a month – twice a year	30% (10)	36% (40)	39% (11)	43% (3)	11% (1)	50% (9)	57% (4)	21% (10)	53% (9)
Once a year or less	39% (13)	32% (35)	29% (8)	—	56% (5)	33% (6)	—	50% (24)	29% (5)
Total	(33)	(110)	(28)	(7)	(9)	(18)	(7)	(48)	(17)

B = Black
W = White
H = Hispanic
Missing observations = 11

Table 2.6

Frequency Of Seeing Children
(By Ethnicity and Gender)

	Black		White		Hispanic	
	M	F	M	F	M	F
At least once a week	57% (4)	33% (13)	36% (14)	29% (37)	33% (7)	19% (8)
A few times a month – twice a year	29% (2)	36% (14)	10% (4)	37% (47)	33% (7)	51% (22)
Once a year or less	14% (1)	31% (12)	54% (21)	34% (43)	33% (7)	30% (13)
Total	(7)	(39)	(39)	(127)	(21)	(43)

M = Male
F = Female
Missing observations = 12

When these respondents were asked, "In some emergency, can you depend on children, their spouses, or a close friend to help you?" nearly two-thirds indicated having one or more persons to help in an emergency, whether these be their own offspring or close friends. Analyzing these data in terms of ethnicity, we obtain the following information:

Table 2.7

In Some Emergency, Can You Depend On Children, Their Spouses, Or Close Friends To Help You?
(By Ethnicity)

	Black	White	Hispanic	Total
Definitely yes	82% (54)	59% (153)	63% (58)	64% (265)
Possibly yes – Definitely no	18% (12)	41% (104)	37% (34)	36% (150)
Total	(66)	(257)	(92)	(415)
Percent	16%	62%	22%	100%

Missing observations = 9

These data show that the Blacks are about half as likely as Whites or Hispanics to believe they are unlikely to get help from family or friends in an emergency (18% compared to 41% and 37% respectively). This is clearly related to the greater frequency of contact between Blacks and their children.

When questioned about ability to depend on children, their spouses, or a close friend to help in an emergency, the analysis in terms of ethnicity was the following:

Table 2.8

If You Need Help For A Longer Period, Can You Depend On Your Children, Their Spouses, Or A Close Friend To Help You?
(By Ethnicity)

	Black	White	Hispanic	Total
Definitely yes	72%	48%	50%	52%
	(47)	(122)	(46)	(215)
Unlikely – No	28%	53%	50%	48%
	(18)	(134)	(46)	(198)
Total	(65)	(156)	(92)	(413)
Percent	16%	62%	22%	100%

Missing observations = 11

The data show that only about half of the elderly within this sample feel "definitely" or "probably" that help would be available to them for an indefinite period of time if they were in such need. However, an important aspect of this analysis is that Blacks are clearly more confident of receiving longer periods of assistance than are Whites or Hispanics.

Respondents were asked where their children lived. The information is presented in the following series of tables.

Table 2.9a

Where Does Your Child Live?
(By Ethnicity and Age: Respondents Age 65–71)

	Black	White	Hispanic	Total
With respondent	— —	14% (4)	17% (4)	12% (8)
Metropolitan area	92% (11)	28% (8)	37% (9)	43% (28)
Away from NYC	8% (1)	59% (17)	46% (11)	45% (29)
Total	(12)	(29)	(24)	(65)
Percent	18%	45%	37%	100%

Table 2.9b

Where Does Your Child Live?
(By Ethnicity and Age: Respondents Age 72–76)

	Black	White	Hispanic	Total
With respondent	13% (2)	6% (2)	37% (7)	16% (11)
Metropolitan area	33% (5)	47% (17)	26% (5)	39% (27)
Away from NYC	53% (8)	47% (17)	37% (7)	46% (32)
Total	(15)	(36)	(19)	(70)
Percent	21%	51%	27%	100%

Table 2.9c

Where Does Your Child Live?
(By Ethnicity and Age: Respondents Age 77–80)

	Black	White	Hispanic	Total
With	8%	6%	7%	6%
respondent	(1)	(3)	(1)	(5)
Metropolitan	75%	28%	43%	38%
area	(9)	(14)	(6)	(29)
Away from	17%	67%	50%	56%
NYC	(2)	(34)	(7)	(43)
Total	(12)	(51)	(14)	(77)
Percent	16%	66%	18%	100%

Table 2.9d

Where Does Your Child Live?
(By Ethnicity and Age: Respondents Age 81+)

	Black	White	Hispanic	Total
With	33%	2%	—	5%
respondent	(2)	(1)	—	(3)
Metropolitan	33%	50%	50%	48%
area	(2)	(24)	(2)	(28)
Away from	33%	48%	50%	47%
NYC	(2)	(23)	(2)	(27)
Total	(6)	(48)	(4)	(58)
Percent	10%	83%	7%	100%

Table 2.10a

Where Does Your Child Live?
(By Ethnicity and Gender: Men)

	Black	White	Hispanic	Total
With respondent	17% (1)	8% (3)	11% (2)	10% (6)
Metropolitan area	67% (4)	29% (11)	42% (8)	36% (23)
Away from NYC	17% (1)	63% (24)	47% (9)	54% (34)
Total	(6)	(38)	(19)	(63)
Percent	10%	60%	30%	100%

Table 2.10b

Where Does Your Child Live?
(By Ethnicity and Gender: Women)

	Black	White	Hispanic	Total
With respondent	11% (4)	6% (7)	24% (10)	10% (21)
Metropolitan area	58% (22)	41% (50)	32% (13)	42% (85)
Away from NYC	32% (12)	53% (65)	44% (18)	47% (95)
Total	(38)	(122)	(41)	(201)
Percent	19%	61%	20%	100%

Missing observations = 23

These tables serve to inform us that in general, the offspring of the respondents do not live with them. A larger percentage of Hispanics than of Blacks or of Whites reports having children who live with them, while the Blacks tend to have offspring who live either nearby or within the metropolitan area. The children of the White respondents reside, for the most part, beyond the metropolitan area. Therefore, traveling and/or commuting must be taken into consideration by these children if they are summoned for help by their parents.

Within the supportive network involving parents and children, there is often reciprocity, in that there is an exchange of services in times of need.

Table 2.11

If Some Emergency Came Up In The Lives Of
Your Children (Or Close Friend), Is It Likely
That You Would Go And Help Out?
(By Ethnicity)

	Black	White	Hispanic	Total
Very and somewhat likely	73% (49)	45% (114)	61% (55)	53% (218)
Not likely at all	27% (18)	55% (141)	39% (36)	47% (195)
Total	(67)	(255)	(91)	(413)
Percent	16%	62%	22%	100%

Missing observations = 11

Analysis reveals that there is a reciprocal relationship involved within the structural-supportive network of the Blacks and Hispanics, in that both groups responded affirmatively (it is "likely") that they would go out to help their children at a time of need. However, the White group did not indicate a similar strong response of extending such a service. This finding serves to support the research findings presented by Mindel and Hayes, and by Cantor (*loc. cit.*). Therefore, one might assume either that such a reciprocal relationship does not exist, or that they can no longer participate in it due to either transportation or health problems.

Since we have been exploring the structural and reciprocal supportive networking between the elderly and their children, it is also important to examine this type of relationship with members of the extended family.

II. Relative-Kinship Support

In obtaining information on frequency of visiting relatives, it is important to examine this variable from several aspects, namely the number of visitations as influenced by the respondents' gender, age, marital status, and ethnicity. By so doing we can explore another dimension of this network of helping in time of need.

Table 2.12a

Frequency Of Seeing And Visiting Relatives
(By Gender)

	Males	Females	Total
Once a week or more – twice a year	29% (32)	24% (70)	26% (102)
Once a year or less	22% (24)	25% (72)	24% (96)
Never see relatives	50% (57)	50% (142)	50% (199)
Total	(113)	(284)	(397)
Percent	28.5%	71.5%	100%

Missing observations = 27

The analysis and interpretation that we can obtain from this table is that half of these respondents neither visit nor see their relatives. Gender makes no significant difference. Various explanations might be that they (the respondents) live too far a distance from their kin; they might communicate ("visit") with them via telephone; they are too infirm; or they may simply have outlived their relatives. In examining this question by variable of age, we learned the following:

Table 2.12b

Frequency Of Seeing And Visiting Relatives
(By Age)

	65–71	72–76	77–80	81+	Total
Once a week or more – twice a year	35% (33)	27% (29)	21% (21)	22% (22)	26% (105)
Once a year or less	24% (23)	28% (29)	17% (17)	26% (27)	24% (96)
Never see relatives	41% (39)	45% (47)	63% (64)	52% (54)	50% (204)
Total	(95)	(105)	(102)	(103)	(405)
Percent	24%	26%	25%	25%	100%

Missing observations = 19

Table 2.12b indicates that about three-fourths of our respondents have very few or no contacts with their relatives, regardless of age of respondent. One might surmise, however, that the "Young Old" (65–71) and the "Middle-Aged Old" (72–76) are a bit more likely to see relatives because they and their relatives are younger and more mobile.

Table 2.12c

Frequency Of Seeing And Visiting Relatives
(By Ethnicity)

	Black	White	Hispanic	Total
Once a week or more – twice a year	36% (24)	19% (48)	37% (31)	26% (103)
Once a year or less	30% (20)	23% (57)	21% (18)	23% (95)
Never see relatives	34% (23)	58% (143)	42% (36)	51% (202)
Total	(67)	(248)	(85)	(400)
Percent	17%	62%	21%	100%

Missing observations = 24

Table 2.12c informs us that Whites are the most isolated from relatives, reporting the lowest percentage of visitation, and that Blacks are the least isolated from relatives in terms of visitation.

Summary

The supportive literature and statistical tables within this chaper serve to refute many of our myths or stereotypes regarding the importance of ethnicity for the minority elderly. Even though many of the minority elderly have experienced deficits of income, health, and housing — more often than the majority — in their lives, they may or may not receive assistance from children and kin in times of need. The data indicate that the Hispanic elderly are the most likely to have "functional children" with whom they interact frequently and from whom they receive a significant amount of help. It is impossible, however, to predict how long this supportive help might continue, for studies (namely Cantor, *et al.*) have informed us that the Hispanic elderly are particularly affected by strains of bridging the two cultures. It is quite possible that as the current generation of younger Hispanics becomes more acculturated, the previous cultural ties and bonds may not be as strictly adhered to as in the past.

In reference to the Black elderly and their functional supportive network, the hypotheses offered by Mindel and Hayes (*loc. cit.*) with regard to the likelihood of support from children in time of need appear to be correct and corroborated by the findings shown in Tables 2.7 and 2.8. Most research studies seem to reflect the thinking that physical proximity to the children appears to be the more basic and long range determinant in supplying aid. If this holds true, we can expect in the future that ethnicity per se will diminish as a predictor of informal social support.

Within the aspects of functionality as offered by Gibson *et al.* — spouse, child, or kin — the tables support the concept that the availability of a kinship network for both majority and minority elderly continues to be an operative one for persons in times of need, if the family helping network is still intact. If the attachment, protective, and bonding relationships are still in operation, then the dependency needs of the elderly family members will be adequately met, as was suggested by Bowlby *et al.*

One additional finding should be stressed. Although most of the previously cited gerontological literature suggest the existence of a strong kinship-helping network, this sample population has relatively few contacts with their kin (see, for example, Table 2.12), and it is somewhat difficult to give an explanation for this situation.

In the following chapter we wlll attempt to examine these respondents' physical health and abilities to cope with their physical and environmental situations.

The Role of Physical Health

The perception of their health status has an important influence on the ways in which aged persons relate to their social worlds. This situation is particularly significant when it is realized that the overall subjective well-being of elderly adults appears to be closely related to their perceived level of health (Cockerham; Sharp; Wilcox, 1983). A review of the literature reveals that self-assessment of health is the strongest single predictor of life satisfaction among older people (Laison; Myles, 1978; Palmore and Luikart, 1972), and that this association apparently increases with age (Spreitzer and Snyder, 1974).

Some studies have found that self-ratings of health among elderly adults are valid measures of objective health (Ferraro, 1980; Fillenbaum, 1979; Maddox and Douglass, 1973; Palmore and Luikart, 1972; Tissue, 1972). It is a biological fact that one's health deteriorates with age, so it is therefore presumed that elderly people report relatively poor health in general. Such, however, is not the case. Many studies find that both institutionalized and non-institutionalized elderly persons tend to rate their health positively (Ferraro, 1980; Fillenbaum, 1979; Myles, 1978; Rose, 1965; Shanas et al., 1968). Ferraro (1980) found that even the oldest among the elderly (people over 75 — the older-aged old) have been found to express an especially positive view of their own health. However, as Shanas notes, "Old age and illness are not synonymous. There is not such disease as old age . . . , for the elderly [who] are not bedridden nor immobilized" (1968). It has been reported by Cantor and Mayer (1974) that most of the older people in the inner city consider themselves in at least fair health, have a relatively low rate of hospitalization, and continue to perform the tasks of daily living with little or no difficulty. But concern about health and illness are verbalized most frequently as a cause of worry by the elderly living in the inner city. The adequate delivery of health services is essential, not only for their current health status, but as a means of preventing future institutionalization.

In elderly persons' self-assessments of personal health, they often compare themselves with peers of their own age and sex, and take into account expectations others have of their health (Fillenbaum, 1979; Maddox, 1962; Shanas *et al.*, 1968). The tendency of aged persons to rate their health in such fashion apparently stems from two types of rationalization. First, their having survived to old age in a state reasonably free of serious illness or severe disability is evidence of relatively good health (Cockerham *et al.*, 1983), and second, Myles (1978) informs us that subjective responses to a health problem tend to be a function of how much of a person's life is disrupted by the condition. The extent of the potential disruption is determined, in turn, by the level of physical and mental functioning required by the social environment. In general, the elderly are not required to maintain a highly active level of functioning, and thus they find it easier to perceive their health as good enough to meet the needs of their environment. Thus, being alive and able to function adequately serves to promote the subjective impression that one's health is relatively good.

The present research population's self-assessments of health were examined, controlling on several variables.

Table 3.1 reveals that nearly half of the respondents rate their health as "fair," with the others divided almost equally between more positive ratings ("good" and "excellent") and less positive ratings. Gender is apparently unrelated to this measure.

Table 3.1

Self-Evaluation Of health
(By Ethnicity and Gender)

Health Status	Black		White		Hispanic		Total
	Male	Female	Male	Female	Male	Female	
Excellent – good	30%	35%	31%	17%	30%	31%	26%
	(3)	(20)	(24)	(30)	(9)	(19)	(105)
Fair	60%	42%	37%	44%	50%	48%	44%
	(6)	(24)	(29)	(76)	(15)	(30)	(180)
Poor	10%	23%	32%	38%	20%	21%	30%
	(1)	(13)	(25)	(66)	(6)	(13)	(124)
Total	(10)	(57)	(78)	(172)	(30)	(62)	(409)

Missing observations = 15

Table 3.2

Self-Reported Health Status
(By Ethnicity and Age)

Health Status	Black		White		Hispanic		Total
	65–76	77+	65–76	77+	65–76	77+	
Excellent – good	50% (18)	16% (5)	19% (21)	24% (35)	33% (23)	20% (5)	26% (107)
Fair	33% (12)	59% (19)	48% (52)	38% (55)	52% (36)	40% (10)	44% (184)
Poor	17% (6)	25% (8)	33% (36)	38% (56)	15% (10)	40% (10)	30% (126)
Total	(36)	(32)	(109)	(146)	(69)	(25)	(417)

Missing observations = 7

In terms of ethnicity, it is clear that Whites, regardless of gender, are more likely to report lower self-ratings than are either Blacks or Hispanics. Even when age is taken into consideration, as in Table 3.2, Whites between the ages of 65 and 76 are more likely to rate their health as lower than either of the other two ethnic groups; among the older respondents, the difference between Whites and Hispanics disappears, thus highlighting the Blacks' continuing tendency to rate their health more positively.

In addition, it is clear that age is more closely related to self-reported health for Blacks and Hispanics than it is for Whites. In the absence of additional data by which to test any hypotheses as to why this should be so, we can only speculate that there is a kind of reference-group effect at work here (Merton, 1968): the shorter average life span of Blacks and Hispanics may simply promote a greater sense of well-being among those minority group members who survive to age 65 and older.

Marital status does not account for the likelihood that Blacks will give themselves more positive health ratings. As Table 3.3 shows, although the widowed are less optimistic about their health than those in other marital categories, when this factor is combined with ethnicity the relationship between ethnicity and health rating remains unchanged.

Table 3.3

Self-Reported Health Status
(By Ethnicity and Marital Status)

Health Status	Black		White		Hispanic	
	Widowed	Other	Widowed	Other	Widowed	Other
Excellent – good	33% (14)	36% (9)	20% (28)	25% (29)	28% (11)	32% (17)
Fair	46% (20)	44% (11)	39% (55)	44% (51)	46% (18)	49% (26)
Poor	21% (9)	20% (5)	41% (58)	30% (35)	26% (10)	19% (10)
Total	(43)	(25)	(141)	(115)	(39)	(53)

Missing observations = 8

Responses to a question concerning actual health care practices ("How often do you visit the doctor or clinic?") suggest that this variable is not significantly influenced by the respondents' ethnicity, gender, or even age. As shown in Table 3.4a, slightly more than half of them report visiting a doctor or clinic more often than "several times a year," with Whites saying this just a bit more often and Blacks just a bit less often. While these differences are in line with self-reports of health discussed earlier, they are by no means evidence of a meaningful distinction between these categories.

Table 3.4a

Frequency Of Doctor Visitation
(By Ethnicity)

	Black	White	Hispanic	Total
High	52%	57%	55%	
	(36)	(147)	(51)	(234)
Low	48%	43%	45%	(184)
	(33)	(110)	(41)	
Total	100%	100%	100%	100%
	(69)	(257)	(92)	(418)

Missing observations = 6

High Attendance = Persons who reported having gone to the doctor "daily," "several times a week," or "once a month."

Low Attendance = Persons who reported having gone to the doctor "several times a year," "rarely," or "never," or who gave no response.

Table 3.4b reveals no differences at all between the sexes, and Table 3.4c indicates that beyond the age of 71, additional years do not necessarily entail an increased frequency of visiting doctors or clinics.

Table 3.4b

Frequency Of Doctor Visitation
(By Gender, All Groups Combined)

	Male	Female	Total
High	55% (65)	56% (166)	(231)
Low	45% (54)	44% (130)	(184)
Total	100% (119)	100% (296)	100% (415)

Missing observations = 9

High Attendance = Persons who reported having gone to the doctor "daily," "several times a week," or "once a month."

Low Attendance = Persons who reported having gone to the doctor "several times a year," "rarely," or "never," or who gave no response.

Table 3.4c

Frequency Of Doctor Visitation
(By Age)

	65–71	72–76	77–80	80+	Total
High*	49% (50)	60% (66)	55% (57)	58% (62)	(235)
Low*	51% (53)	40% (44)	45% (47)	42% (44)	(188)
Total	100% (103)	100% (110)	100% (104)	100% (106)	100% (423)

* Indicates the *specific* responses that are combined in "high attendance" and "low attendance."

These data are only slightly inconsistent with those given above in Tables 3.1 and 3.2. In the former, females were more likely than males to report their own health as "poor," but the difference was not significant. In the latter, respondents aged 77 and older were very clearly more likely to report "poor" health than those respondents who were younger. But even here, the overall difference between older and younger respondents is only 12 percent.

Finally, in examining the influence of marital status on frequency of visiting a doctor or clinic, the findings given in Table 3.5 supply only limited support for the belief that close ties (that is, living with one's spouse) should be associated with signs of better health.

Table 3.5

Frequency Of Doctor Visits
(By Marital Status, All Groups Combined)

	Single*	Married*	Total #	Total %
Daily	1% (3)	— —	(3)	1%
At least once a week	7% (22)	12% (12)	(34)	8%
At least once a month	49% (156)	41% (41)	(197)	47%
At least once a year	36% (114)	32% (32)	(146)	35%
Rarely**	8% (25)	16% (16)	(41)	9%
Total	(320)	(101)	(421)	
Percent	76%	24%		100%

  * *Single* includes the never-married, widowed, divorced, and separated.

  Married refers to those living with a spouse.

** Only in the case of an emergency.

Indeed, it is only at what can be thought of as the "healthy" end of the scale (visiting a doctor or clinic only in the case of an emergency) that married people exhibit better health than those without spouses. It is likely that this statistical finding, however, is due as much to the fact that our married respondents tend to be younger, as to the benefits derived from the intimacy of marriage.

Summary

This chapter on the health status of the aged population of both minority and majority persons has given us relatively little in the way of differences among our basic demographic categories. It is clear that Whites, regardless of age or marital status, tend to rate themselves lower in self-perceived health than do either Blacks or Hispanics. It may be supposed that this is due to a combination of relatively weaker support networks, since it is the Whites whose children are much more likely to live far away from them, and reference group phenomena, which should make the mere survival of minority group members into old age reason enough for optimism about the state of their health.

Despite being more pessimistic about their health, though, Whites did not appear to use this as a basis for more frequent utilization of health-care facilities. Differences between them and our Black and Hispanic respondents were virtually nonexistent in this regard. This statistical finding can lead us to suspect that self-reports of health status are reflective more of morale than of actual physical condition.

It should be noted, too, that the respondents expressed high satisfactions when asked, "How satisfied are you with the health care you receive?" The researcher examined this variable in terms of ethnicity, age, marital status, and gender. The statistical reporting showed no significant differences within the cross-tabulations. All of the respondents rated the received health care very highly and were satisfied. Since this was the statistical finding for this variable, there was no need to incorporate a chart for illustration. In summation, we can say that our findings served to support the assertion that these respondents are generally high in feelings of control and satisfaction with their destinies and well-being.

Given what is apparently adequate utilization of health-care facilities, we must still remember that the gerontological literature addresses itself to the inability of the minority aged to obtain needed services (Lambrana *et al.*, 1979). This is attributed to their fear of doctors and hospitals, due to past historical and present acts of racism by medical providers. Lambrana (*loc cit.*) further informs us that for some minority aged, cultural healers may affect utilization of the formal health-care system. Many Puerto Ricans, for example, maintain a belief in "espiritisas," who are indigenous folk-healers who mediate between the spiritual realm and human beings. Believers feel that spirits can identify the root cause of a health problem and suggest solutions to alleviate the problem.

The largest problem in health status, care, and utilization is the situation of fragmentation and depersonalization of services which affect both the minority and the majority aged. Cantor (1974) describes depersonalization or long waiting hours, inconvenient hours of service, the confusing atmosphere of large busy clinics, and the insensitivity of doctors and nurses who lack the opportunity to develop an ongoing relationship with individual patients. Thus the elderly poor are particularly vulnerable in such a system. In this next chapter, we will address ourselves to the frequency of use of agency programs and community services by the elderly, and the types of agencies they use.

Social Agency Utilization

Relationships to Helping Agencies

Existing service systems are mostly inadequate and inappropriate to the needs of the elderly. It is therefore necessary to examine the requirements of those who are being served and of those who are not, so as to modify existing patterns of service delivery, and to create new systems tailored to those requirements.

King (1983) informs us that those in the greatest need, yet possessing the least power and means to improve their quality of life, tend to get the most ineffective responses from society. In terms of the elderly population, this tendency has been documented since the colonial period (Kutznik, 1979). It has been reported that during that time, services for the needs of the elderly were so inadequate and misguided that many were placed in institutions, along with the mentally impaired, criminals, and orphans — thus the creation of the poorhouse.

Many socio-demographic studies conducted on the service needs of the elderly indicate that they struggle through their last years in circumstances characterized by inadequacies — of income, housing, medical care, and many other basic aspects of life. These circumstances and conditions are compounded for the elderly of minority groups. It has been stated that for them, "the atrocities suffered throughout life are simply amplified in old age" (King, *op. cit.*).

Cantor (1975), in her study of "Utilization of Services by Urban Elderly," argues that older people are fiercely

independent and that their response to services indicates
that in most cases their initial reaction is to try to manage
on their own or, if necessary, turn to the members of the
informal support system with whom they have a primary
relationship, such as a child, an intimate, or a neighbor.
Community agencies are referred to primarily when
personal or family resources are exhausted or nonexistent,
or when the type of assistance required is beyond the
capacity of the informal support system. In particular, these
tend to be agencies responsible for providing the basic floor
of income maintenance and health entitlements —
principally the Social Security Administration and the
Department of Human Resources.

With regard to this aspect of old age, the respondents
were asked, "How often do you go to governmental
agencies, such as Social Security, Medicare, or Medicaid
offices?" Here the researcher was concerned with how
often the respondents had to interact with these
governmental agencies.

Table 4.1

Frequency Of Going To Governmental Agencies

	Absolute	Percent
Monthly	2	*
Occasionally	27	7
Rarely	51	13
Never	315	80
Total	395	100%

* Less than 1%

Missing observations = 29

The information that we obtain from Table 4.1 is that
80 percent of this population of elderly persons (the
Easyriders) never go to any governmental helping agency.
Seemingly, their needs are being met adequately so there is

no need for such visitations. Thus, this tendency to perceive community resources as a secondary source of support and this relatively low level of utilization of governmental agencies by this group of elderly becomes clearer.

The Role and Function of Services Utilization

The examination of factors that affect service utilization must focus on what elements or combination of elements inhibit or facilitate service utilization. The previous chapters of this study, on social support networks and health services, have generated additional reason to look into this topic.

In a study conducted by Watson *et al.* (1981) regarding minority elders' use of agency services, the investigators found that the Black elderly reportedly feared the loss of their Social Security if they participated in agency services. Watson and his colleagues also reported that many minority elderly members had refused Social Security benefits. Other researchers (Bell, Kasschau, and Zellman, 1976) have presented similar findings, reporting that people sometimes fail to apply for services because of fears that the government may intrude in their personal lives.

The Senior Centers

Harris (1981) informs us that attendance at senior centers has risen steadily since a previous study in 1974, and that there is indication of increased interest in and usage of these centers in the future. Harris further argues that the proportion of older Americans attending senior citizens' centers is related positively to age. Only 5 percent of those aged 65 to 69, as compared to 21 percent of those 70 years old and older, have attended a senior center. Further, regardless of age, women participate in the activities of these centers more than men do, and are more likely to show interest in doing so in the future. Within the minority classification, Blacks as a group show the greatest interest in senior centers — 43 percent of those aged 55 and over who do not now attend them would like to.

Demko's study (1977) of users of senior centers informs us that utilization is related to social losses and gains, indicating the significance of need states among the elderly, along with differences in perceived life space, club affiliation, number of friends, and living arrangements.

Trinidad and Borg (1976), in their examination of a sample of Puerto Ricans, found the existence of a trusting relationship between service providers and clients to be of primary importance in utilization.

Within the framework of this study pertaining to the utilization of senior centers, respondents were asked, "How often do you go to the senior center?"

Table 4.2

Frequency Of Going To The Senior Center

	Absolute	Percent
Daily	55	14
Several times a week	67	17
Monthly	36	9
Occasionally	33	8
Never	206	52
Total	397	100%

Missing observations = 27

Table 4.2 suggests that about half of these respondents never go to the senior centers while about one-third go at least once a week. (However, see the caveat below.)

The senior centers have structured and developed many vital-linkage programs for the participants within their communities. One of the most beneficial has been the daily hot meal. When the respondents were asked, "Do you ever go to the senior center for lunch?" we learned the following:

Table 4.3

Frequency Of Going To The Senior Center For Lunch
(By Age)

	65–76	77+
Daily	20% (41)	27% (57)
Several times a week	60% (127)	55% (115)
Rarely or never	20% (42)	17% (36)
Total	100% (210)	99% (208)

Missing observations = 6

Table 4.3 informs us that most of the aged within this study do utilize the senior center for the lunch program. Seemingly, most of the respondents attended at least several times a week, if not daily. This is in apparent contradiction to the replies received when respondents were asked how often they go to the senior center (see Table 4.2). Fifty-two percent indicated that they never go to the senior center, and yet 83 percent (340) said that they go to the senior center for lunch at least several times a week, and only 17 percent (78) eat there "rarely or never." It may be suggested that this discrepancy arises from interpretation of the original question, "How often do you go to the Senior Center?" The two sets of apparently contradictory figures raise the suspicion that the original question was interpreted as meaning "How often do you go to the Senior Center for anything besides a meal?"

With these reported frequencies, respondents were asked whether they were satisfied or dissatisfied with the agency (senior center).

Table 4.4

Satisfaction With The Senior Center
(By Gender)

	Men	Women	Total
Very Satisfied	69% (59)	73% (165)	72% (224)
Both somewhat satisfied/somewhat dissatisfied	18% (15)	16% (35)	16% (50)
Very dissatisfied	13% (11)	11% (25)	12% (36)
Total	29% (85)	71% (225)	100% (310)

Missing observations = 114

Table 4.4 serves to support the finding that both male and female respondents report being "very satisfied" with services provided at the senior center.

In examining this variable as to those persons who might or might not have family, we obtained the following information:

Table 4.5

Frequency Of Going To The Senior Center For Lunch
(By Cohabitation)

	Live Alone	Live With Someone
Daily	37% (79)	14% (19)
Several times a week	32% (70)	54% (71)
Rarely or never	30% (67)	32% (42)
Total	100% (216)	100% (132)

Table 4.5 informs us that those persons who "live alone" and are without close family members are the most frequent utilizers of the hot lunch program. This again demonstrates the continuous need for "congregate meal sites" for this population of frequent utilizers, composed primarily of widowed and never-married persons.

In examining this variable in terms of ethnicity, we learned the following information:

Table 4.6

Frequency Of Going To The Senior Center For Lunch
(By Ethnicity)

	Black	White	Hispanic	Total
Daily	23% (16)	26% (66)	15% (14)	23% (96)
Several times a week	65% (44)	53% (137)	63% (58)	57% (239)
Rarely or never	12% (8)	20% (54)	23% (22)	20% (84)
Total	16% (68)	61% (257)	22% (94)	100% (419)

Missing observations = 5

Table 4.6 informs us that the minorities within this population utilize this nutrition program as frequently as do the whites. The data show that a larger proportion of the Blacks than of the Hispanics are involved daily. The reasons can be manifold, although the information earlier given by Trinidad and Borg (1976, *op. cit.*) may explain why the Hispanics are less likely to utilize agency services. These authors maintain that an emotional climate of trust and warmth is of primary importance in utilization of agency services by Puerto Ricans.[1]

The Role of the Church as Helping Agent

Cantor (1975) agrees that religious institutions play an important part in the lives of many inner-city elderly, particularly the Blacks and Hispanics. She maintains that they frequently turn for assistance to religious leaders, including spiritualists. Therefore, it was difficult for her to distinguish between occasions in which the elderly actually asked for assistance, and those that were part of ongoing involvement with religious institutions.

The research here will address itself to the frequencies of attendance in terms of gender, age, categorization, and ethnicity. The relationship between religious practices and the aging process serves to raise the themes of confronting the crisis of late life (impending death) and patterns of participation throughout the life cycle.

In examining the data regarding these issues, we were able to obtain the following:

Table 4.7a

Frequency Of Church Attendance
(By Gender)

	Men	Women
Once a week or more	26% (30)	29% (84)
Several times a month – several times a year	23% (26)	29% (85)
Rarely or never	51% (59)	42% (124)
Total	28% (115)	72% (293)

Missing observations = 16

In examining Table 4.7a, we again see that women are slightly more likely to attend church services and/or programs. It is more striking, however, that half of the men and more than 40 percent of the women report attending only rarely or never.

We examined church attendance by age categorization, and found that age has a marked effect upon the frequency of attendance (see Table 4.7b).

Table 4.7b

Frequency Of Church Attendance
(By Age)

	65–76	77+
Once a week or more	34% (70)	22% (46)
Several times a month – several times a year	31% (63)	24% (50)
Rarely or never	35% (73)	54% (112)
Total	(206)	(208)

Table 4.6b informs us that church attendance changes rather sharply after age 77, in that there is a sharp decline, although one-fifth of those over 77 do still manage to get to services at least once a week.

In examining the question of church attendance by ethnicity (Table 4.7c), we see that aged Blacks are more frequent attendees at church services than are aged Whites, and that the Hispanic respondents (who are most likely to be of the Catholic faith) attend church most frequently.

Table 4.7c

Frequency Of Church Attendance
(By Ethnicity)

	Black	White	Hispanic
Once a week or more	33% (22)	20% (52)	44% (39)
Several times a month – several times a year	30% (20)	28% (70)	25% (22)
Rarely or never	37% (25)	52% (132)	31% (27)
Total	16% (67)	62% (254)	22% (88)

Missing observations = 15

The results of this analysis indicate that religion and religious service attendance continue to be an important activity for the elderly, even in later life. Although almost half report attending rarely or never, data are not available as to whether they are involved with religiously oriented radio and television broadcasts. Some researchers, namely Burgess (1950), inform us that decreased church attendance among the aged is more than offset by increases in the amount of time they spend listening to the radio and often in private Bible reading. A similar research finding was confirmed by Toch (1953), that private prayer and Bible reading increase with advancing age.

Mindel and Vaugham (1978) maintain that such findings suggest the necessity of conceptualizing older persons' religious practices in multi-dimensional terms so as to avoid the mistaken conclusion that religion is somehow less salient in later life. Another aspect of their discussion of disengagement theory is the thought that one surrenders many responsible social roles upon reaching a certain age and stage of life.

Harris (1974) maintains that attendance at a church or synagogue is slightly higher among the older public than among those under 65. He further states that attendance is lowest among the very young, peaks among those 55 to 79, and falls off somewhat among those 80 and over. Harris feels that while attendance at a house of worship does not increase steadily with age, the importance which people attach to religion in their lives does. He reports that 71 percent of the public 65 and over feel that religion is very important in their own lives, as compared with only 49 percent of those under age 65.

In summation, the findings reported in this chapter as to the reported frequencies with which the aged utilize helping agencies may or may not be an adequate indication of their need for governmental and/or non-governmental agency services. Some older people have needs over and above those dealt with by the designated agencies. Others might not know where to go to match their needs with the appropriate service provider. Seemingly, those agencies that are used for whatever type of service request are well utilized. It will thus remain for the following chapter to report and assess the unmet needs of this elderly population.

Summary

This chapter has examined the research population's involvement with three distinct types of formal helping agencies: major governmental agencies such as Social Security and Medicaid, local senior citizens centers, and religious groups.

With regard to the first of these, the finding that fully 80 percent of the respondents "never go" to any of these agencies may mask the frequency with which their services are used indirectly. We know from Chapter 1, certainly, that virtually the entire research population has some involvement with the Social Security Administration (Table

1.9), and we can be nearly as certain that a large majority enjoy some type of Medicare or Medicaid benefits.

Where senior citizen centers are concerned, if our interpretation of the apparent discrepancy between Tables 4.2 and 4.3 is acceptable, we can reason that about four-fifths of the respondents utilize their lunch services and that about half make use of other services offered by the centers.

Finally, we find that about 45 percent of our respondents attend religious services "rarely or never," and that this figure rises with the age of the respondents. It is likely, further, that the higher frequencies of attendance reported by Blacks and Hispanics are due mainly to their relatively lower ages and the greater likelihood that the Hispanics in particular are Catholic rather than Protestant or Jewish.

The picture is thus clouded as to whether "adequate" services are provided by these agencies. Some older people have needs over and above those dealt with by the designated agencies. Others might not know where to go to match their needs with the appropriate service provider. It must thus remain for the following chapter to report and assess the unmet needs of this elderly population.

Notes

[1] Thus the senior center programs, which are administered by the Bureau of Purchased Special Services (BPSS), continues to provide social group services, meals, recreation, counseling, and a variety of other services to persons 60 years old and older. Despite inflation and a decrease in federal funding, the senior centers continue to provide a unique mechanism for meeting the social and nutritional needs of older citizens. Family and Adult Services (FAS) directly operates 64 senior

centers and submitted 74 contracts to the Board of Estimate for approval for fiscal year 1985. These contracts represent 116 programs serving meals and protective services (Gross, 1985). Table 4.5 provides an analysis of cost and management of operational expense for the New York City Senior Center hot lunch program (1985).

Life Satisfaction: Morale, Well-Being, and Life Expectations

This chapter will address itself to the quality of life satisfactions of the respondents — namely, their morale and overall well-being and life expectations. These concepts have long played an important role in social gerontology, and are often used as interchangeable terms for a general set of concerns (Cutler, 1978). Measures of the concepts have most typically been used as dependent variables in efforts to trace the impact of specified life-course changes upon aging adults (for example, residential changes, widowhood, and decrements in health or well-being). Psychological measurements also have been developed for purposes of assessment.

While the range of variables that influence life satisfaction may be quite broad, Donnenworth, *et al.* (1978) report that two significant variables influencing life satisfaction have remained relatively obscure. These variables are residence (rural or urban) and race. Some scholars have argued that urban residence, particularly in deteriorating neighborhoods, has a negative effect on life satisfaction or sense of well-being (Lawson and Kleban, 1971; Lawton and Cohen, 1974). However, it has also been argued that the aged in rural areas experience more isolation from relatives and friends (Philblad and McNamara, 1965), and subsequently are likely to have lower life satisfaction. Bultena (1969) reported that the urban elderly have significantly more interaction with their children than do the rural elderly. Jackson (1971) has indicated that race has received relatively little research attention, and that the research findings that do exist with respect to race are frequently contradictory. Apparently no existing study has examined the effects of both residence and race. The research reported here attempts to investigate the effects of ethnicity on life satisfaction among older persons within the urban community.

Life Satisfaction in Relation to the Environment

With regard to other components of life satisfaction, previous research has examined the attitudes of older persons toward their environment (neighborhood) because the environment can very often influence a person's overall emotional well-being.

> Gerontologists are becoming increasingly concerned with the total living environment. They say that the features of the residential area and the surrounding community can determine whether the older person is going to be happy. Since older people are typically in their homes many more hours a day, it's all the more important that their living environment contributes to a full and meaningful life (Barrow and Smith, 1983: 192).

It has been argued that satisfaction with life is one of the major psychological adjustments associated with the aging process, in that aging is related to an increasing dissatisfaction with one's social environment (Alston and Dudley, 1973). Thus, one aspect of mental health is the degree to which the individual successfully adjusts to the changes forced upon him or her with the advent of old age. This difficulty of adjustment has resulted in several major socio-gerontological arguments, namely, those theories dealing with alienation (Dean, 1961; Israel, 1971; Seeman, 1959) and disengagement (Cummings and Henry, 1961). These concepts are of particular interest when examining the relationship between the aging experience and how the person continuously re-evaluates his or her environment. One assumes that successful adjustment particularly involves being able to enjoy one's past, present, and future experiences in the face of aging.

Within this context, we will examine the relationship between the variables of life satisfaction by the identification of those factors which are associated with changes in a person's interest with his home and social surroundings (neighborhood).

In the respondents' responses to the question, "How satisfied are you with your housing?" and controlling for ethnicity, we obtained the following information:

Table 5.1

Satisfaction With Housing
(By Ethnicity)

	Black	White	Hispanic	Total
Very satisfied	90% (61)	95% (243)	94% (88)	(392)
Unsure	2% (1)	* (2)	2% (2)	(5)
Very dissatisfied	9% (6)	5% (12)	4% (4)	(22)
Total	16% (68)	61% (257)	22% (94)	100% (419)

* Less than 1%

The data suggest that our informants are very satisfied with their housing. The variable was examined by both age and marital status, and no significant differences can be reported. Thus, the respondents' high life satisfaction relating to their housing can be attributed to having good health, continuous meaningful social contacts, and/or partners. This information has been reported in earlier chapters of this study, named in Chapters Two and Three,

where we examined the respondents' supportive networks
and their physical health.

In asking the question, "Are you satisfied or dissatisfied
with the neighborhood in which you live?" and controlling
for ethnicity, we obtained the information displayed in
Table 5.2.

Table 5.2

Satisfaction With Neighborhood
(By Ethnicity)

	Black	White	Hispanic	Total
Very satisfied	79% (54)	75% (192)	88% (83)	(329)
Unsure	7% (5)	6% (16)	4% (4)	(25)
Very dissatisfied	14% (9)	19% (49)	8% (7)	(65)
Total	16% (68)	61% (257)	22% (94)	100% (419)

Missing observations = 5

Table 5.2 informs us that more than three-fourths of the
respondents are "very satisfied" with the neighborhoods in
which they live. The Hispanics report even greater
satisfaction than the Blacks do, which may be attributed to
their being the most recently arrived group (historically
speaking) to public housing. Those who report the highest
amount of dissatisfaction with their neighborhoods are the
Whites. This might be explained by their having to remain
in neighborhoods (environments) that have undergone
significant transitions. Possibly, too, they may have lost
previous ties within the neighborhood, which would
diminish the feeling of "belonging." In examining the
variable of neighborhood (environment) satisfaction by age,
marital status, and gender, we learned that the majority of
the respondents are "very satisfied" with their respective

neighborhoods, regardless of differences in these three categories. As reported earlier in Chapter One, this population of persons lived in various sections of the boroughs of Manhattan and the Bronx.

In this cursory explanation of the major ascriptive characteristics of our sample population which might be correlated with satisfaction with the environment, we found little meaningful relationship between it and age, gender, or marital status. With regard to ethnicity, the Whites registered the highest level of dissatisfaction with their neighborhoods, which we interpret as the consequence of their being the earliest to arrive in them and thus to have experienced, collectively, the greatest sense of change and loss.

The following section focuses on a particularly sensitive aspect of the environment — crime.

Life Satisfaction and Fear of Crime

Here we further examine the independent variable life satisfaction, and its relation to crime against the elderly in our society, which is an ever-present fear. Lawton and Yaffe (1980), in their study of "Victimization and Fear of Crime in Elderly Public Housing Tenants," discussed the issue that the fear of crime is very high among the elderly, and that this fear is greatest among women, blacks, the poor, and those living alone both in suburban and urban communities. It has been stated frequently that many of the elderly are "prisoners in their homes" (Conklin, 1976). Thus, this may explain the reasons why the elderly limit their travel and avoid certain areas within their locales. When we asked the population of our study, "Do you worry about getting mugged in the day?" we examined the variable in terms of ethnicity and obtained the information given in Table 5.3a.

Table 5.3a

Fear Of Being Mugged During The Day
(By Ethnicity)

	Black	White	Hispanic	Total
Never	49%	40%	49%	
	(33)	(103)	(46)	(182)
Sometimes	25%	32%	29%	
	(17)	(82)	(27)	(126)
Often	27%	28%	22%	
	(18)	(72)	(21)	(111)
Total	100%	100%	100%	
	(68)	(25)	(94)	(419)

Missing observations = 5

Table 5.3a informs us that the minority respondents — Blacks and Hispanics — are more likely than the White respondents to "never" seem to worry about getting mugged in the daytime. In further examining this variable by age and marital status, we obtained no significant differences. However, in examining the variable by gender, we see that the female respondents rather than the male respondents are the more fearful of being victims of such a crime.

Table 5.3b

Fear Of Being Mugged During The Day
(By Gender)

	Male	Female	Total
Never	52% (62)	40% (119)	(181)
Sometimes	22% (26)	33% (98)	(124)
Often	26% (31)	27% (79)	(110)
Total	100% (119)	100% (296)	(415)

Missing observations = 9

Table 5.3b provides support for the obvious fact that males rather than females receive lifelong preparation to defend themselves and to deny fearfulness. This finding further serves to report the research of Lawton and Jaffe (1980, *loc. cit*).

In summary, the mugging (crime) variable showed that the respondents' overall scores reflect a non-fearfulness of this act of crime within their respective geographical locales. This serves to further enhance their sense of autonomy and life satisfaction. This also can be attributed to already mentioned factors, namely their age, connectedness, and gender (sex). However, another possible contributor to this high rate of satisfaction could be the presence of a Housing Police Force that is assigned to public housing sites. They serve as a deterrent to environmental crimes — daytime muggings. There is also at times a tenant surveillance force in operation in most public housing, thereby offering residents both formal and informal protection.

The variable of morale is generally considered to be the emotional component of life satisfaction, although the two terms have been used interchangeably (Chown, 1977).

Researchers have used it to test early theories in gerontology, such as disengagement and activity theories, as well as the effects that changes in health, marital status, or income might have. Their findings have indicated that in relation to health, those persons with poor health scores have lowered levels of morale and life satisfaction, while those with good health are likely to have higher levels of morale and life satisfaction (Streib and Schneider, 1971; Palmore and Kivett, 1977; Wolk and Telleen, 1976; Ball, Auroin, and Klemmark, 1973; Toseland and Sykes, 1977; Markides and Martin, 1979). Researchers testing activity theory have found that the elderly who continue with middle-aged activities have high morale (Anderson, 1967; Kutner, 1956; Lipman and Smith, 1968; Maddox, 1965; Phillips, 1969; Tobin and Neugarten, 1961; Zeborowski and Eyde, 1962). On the contrary, the disengagement theorists (Cumming, *et al.*, 1960) maintain that factors such as poor health, mandatory retirement, lack of transportation, or widowhood negatively affect morale. In addition, several other factors have also been found to be related to morale among the elderly, including their socio-economic standing, supports, and having a safe environment (Chown, 1977; Wolk and Telleen, 1976; Smith and Lipman, 1972).

Composite Measures of Life Satisfaction

So far, we have examined the respondents of this Easyride study primarily in terms of statistical cross-tabulations and, for the most part, we have not found any significant statistical differences between minority and majority elderly. In trying to make sense out of the data, one conclusion has been that most of the variables were categorical in nature and not readily amenable to more cogent and robust statistical analyses. Since there were some substantive findings that were strongly supported by the research in the field, a new tactic was needed. Thus the researcher then moved to utilize an exploratory factor analysis. Its major purpose is to summarize the information contained in a number of original variables into a smaller set of new latent variables with a minimum of loss of the information contained in a number of original variables. This removes redundancy in the original data as well as reducing the clutter of variables to a more manageable number. The factor scales that will be examined here are those of trust, optimism, and anxiety. The statistical procedures are to be found in Appendix A. These factoral scales (trust, optimism, and anxiety) were also examined and controlled for by ethnicity, by marital status, by age, and by gender.

Table 5.4

Distribution Of Factor Scale Loadings

I. Composite Index — Trust	Factor Loadings
A. Trust	-0.76458
B. Selfish	-0.81323
C. Count on	-0.73526

II. Composite Index — Optimism	Factor Loadings
A. Happy	0.53909
B. Social life	0.76775
C. Grow old	0.68095

III. Composite Index — Anxiety	Factor Loadings
A. Meals	0.77751
B. Housework	0.70019
C. Going out of doors	0.80146

In addition, we combined and collapsed both minority groups (Blacks and Hispanics) into one category in order to determine if their combination would yield statistical significance. The same procedure was utilized for the marital status and age categories.

The Composite Index of Trust is based on attitudes and feelings of allowing oneself to have a sense of trust, giving, and relying on others at a time of need (inter-dependence). The Composite Index of Optimism and the variables composing it are based on self-reported attitudes of feeling happy, satisfaction with one's social life, and one's expectations about growing old. The Scale of Anxiety, and the variables therein, attempted to examine the elderly person's ability to prepare his or her own meals, to do his or her own housework, and to go out (travel, mobility).

All of these factor scales serve to address the elderly person's sense of autonomy, self-control, and freedom from restraints in having to rely on others. As mentioned earlier in this chapter, an individual's life-satisfaction is dependent on these activities, that is, freedom from mental and physical anxieties. In examining these factor scales while controlling on ethnicity, marital status, age, and gender, we were able to learn the following information.

Table 5.5a

Composite Index Of "Trust"
(By Ethnicity and Marital Status)

Trust	Minority (Blacks & Hispanics)		Majority (Whites)		Total
	Married	Single*	Married	Single*	
High	51% (18)	33% (41)	45% (29)	42% (81)	41% (169)
Low	49% (17)	67% (84)	55% (35)	58% (111)	59% (247)
Total	100% (35)	100% (125)	100% (64)	100% (192)	100% (416)

Missing observations = 8

* Never married, separated, divorced, widowed

Table 5.5a suggests that the absence of a spouse has a somewhat greater effect on the overall "trust" of minority persons than on that of the White majority. While the variation between married and non-married whites is virtually non-existent, that between married and non-married minority group members is significant at the .05 level (df = 1, 2 = 4.09, p < .05). This finding seems to emphasize the greater reliance of elderly minority persons on informal support networks such as are provided by the family. The fact that minority females score much lower on the "Trust" scale than minority males (as shown in Table 5.5b) probably only confirms our interpretation of Table 5.5a, since it is the females who are much more likely to be non-married at this period of their lives.

Table 5.5b

Composite Index Of "Trust"
(By Ethnicity and Gender)

Trust	Minority		Majority		
	Males	Females	Males	Females	Total
High	50% (20)	35% (41)	45% (35)	42% (73)	43% (169)
Low	50% (20)	65% (78)	55% (43)	58% (101)	57% (242)
Total	100% (40)	100% (119)	100% (78)	100% (174)	100% (411)

Missing observations = 13

In examining the composite index of "Trust," controlling for ethnicity by age category, we find the following:

Table 5.5c

Composite index Of "Trust"
(By Ethnicity and Age)

Respondents Age 65–76

Trust	Minority	Majority	Total
High	43% (45)	47% (51)	45% (96)
Low	57% (60)	53% (58)	55% (118)
Total	100% (105)	100% (109)	100% (214)

Respondents Age 77–96

Trust	Minority	Majority	Total
High	28% (16)	40% (59)	37% (75)
Low	72% (41)	60% (89)	63% (130)
Total	100% (57)	100% (148)	100% (205)

Missing observations = 5

In examining the composite index of "Trust" by ethnicity and age classifications, we have recorded that the minority respondents in the older and frail elderly classification expressed the lowest score within the composite index of trust. Since the minority respondents in this study tend to be younger than the White respondents (65 percent are below the age of 76, as compared to only 42 percent of the Whites), it is quite likely that older minority members find themselves more socially isolated than their White counterparts. This, we can assume, accounts for the lower "trust" scores recorded for minority respondents in Table 5.5c.

In examining the composite index of "Optimism" and the selected variables therein we were exploring the respondents' attitude in terms of expressed feelings of happiness, satisfaction with one's social life, and one's life expectations in growing old. In doing a cross-tabular analysis controlling for ethnicity by marital status, by gender, and by age, we were able to learn the following:

Table 5.6a

Composite Index Of "Optimism"
(By Ethnicity and Marital Status)

	Married		
Optimism	Minority	Majority	Total
Low	49% (17)	70% (45)	63% (62)
High	51% (18)	30% (19)	37% (37)
Total	100% (35)	100% (64)	100% (99)

	Single*		
Optimism	Minority	Majority	Total
Low	60% (75)	72% (139)	67% (214)
High	40% (50)	28% (53)	33% (103)
Total	100% (125)	100% (192)	100% (317)

* Never married, widowed, divorced, separated

Missing observations = 8

Table 5.6a serves to inform us that the elderly minority respondents — both married and non-married — report a higher score of being happy and satisfied with their social

lives along with their expectations of growing old, whereas
we see that their majority counterparts, both married and
non-married, expressed lower scores. In attempting to
explain the reasons for this occurrence for the majority
respondents, we might say that they have expressed less
optimism because of their reduced social status.

In examining this composite index of "Optimism" and
controlling for ethnicity and gender, we were able to learn
that the higher optimism expressed by minority members is
not affected by gender. (See Table 5.6b.)

Table 5.6b

Composite Index Of "Optimism"
(By Ethnicity and Gender)

Optimism	Minority		Majority		
	Males	Females	Males	Females	Total
Low	58% (23)	58% (69)	68% (53)	74% (128)	65% (273)
High	42% (17)	42% (50)	32% (25)	26% (46)	35% (138)
Total	100% (40)	100% (119)	100% (78)	100% (174)	100% (411)

Missing observations = 13

Table 5.6b informs us that the majority respondents,
especially the women, are less optimistic than the minority
respondents about their happiness, social lives, and their
growing old. When the factor of age is considered as well,
Table 5.6c, we find that it exerts additional influence. The
older Whites, those 77 and older, reveal the lowest degree
of optimism.

Table 5.6c

Composite Index Of "Optimism"
(By Ethnicity and Age)

Respondents Age 65–76

Optimism	Minority	Majority	Total
Low	55% (58)	65% (71)	60% (129)
High	45% (47)	35% (38)	40% (85)
Total	100% (105)	100% (109)	100% (214)

Respondents Age 77–96

Optimism	Minority	Majority	Total
Low	61% (35)	76% (113)	72% (148)
High	39% (22)	24% (35)	28% (57)
Total	100% (57)	100% (148)	100% (205)

Missing observations = 5

Table 5.6c informs us that a majority of the elderly —
regardless of age category — expressed low optimism.
Indeed, the older and frail aged were even more likely than
the young and middle-aged old to score low. However, a

sizable minority of both age categories scored high. This low score on optimism could be attributed to their reduced social status and dissatisfactions with their social life, happiness, and to anxieties about growing old. This could reduce the aged person's life satisfactions and morale.

The "Anxiety Factor Scale" is based on whether the respondent can prepare his or her own meals, do housework, and can go out. All of these factors mainly reflect the state of the respondent's physical health and mobility. Table 5.7 displays the findings with respect to ethnicity and marital status.

Table 5.7

Composite Index Of "Anxiety"
(By Ethnicity and Marital Status)

| | Minority | | Majority | | |
Anxiety	Married	Single*	Married	Single*	Total
High	29%	46%	44%	47%	42%
	(10)	(57)	(29)	(90)	(185)
Low	71%	54%	56%	53%	58%
	(25)	(68)	(36)	(102)	(231)
Total	100%	100%	100%	100%	100%
	(35)	(125)	(64)	(192)	(416)

Missing observations = 8

* Never married, separated, divorced, widowed

Table 5.7 informs us that the aged respondents who continue to be married (i.e., who have a living spouse) express the lowest scores on the composite index of anxiety. Married minority respondents expressed a lower score than their majority counterparts as it again relates to the mutual supportive functional spouse as was reported by the researchers Mindel and Hayes and by Gibson, and in Chapter 2 of this study. Again, a functional spouse is one with whom one lives. This concept of functionality also applies to children and to relatives.

When examining the composite index of anxiety, and controlling for ethnicity by gender and by age, the respondents reported low anxiety scores, and no statistically significant differences appeared.

Summary

In having examined the variables and composite indices that contribute to and measure a person's quality of life, particularly for the aged persons in our society, we have seen within this population that they have expressed a feeling of high satisfaction with their housing and environment (neighborhood). This finding could be attributed to their being in good physical health, as was documented in Chapter 3 of this study. We might also deduce that their life satisfaction could be attributed to their high feelings of optimism and morale. They therefore feel relatively free of many fears and anxieties that might serve to reduce their feelings of autonomy and life satisfaction. Apparently, they (the Easyriders) have a strong sense of self-esteem, self-worth, and futurity. The minority respondents expressed a higher sense of self-satisfaction than their majority counterparts. This might be explained by and attributed to their having survived many life-threatening situations, such as poor health care, poor housing, and limited income.

Summary and Conclusions

The research reported here has been an inquiry into the conditions of urban, low-income, elderly persons. It is concerned basically with three ethnic categories — Black, Hispanic, and White — and with their social-support networks, health status, utilization of governmental and voluntary agencies, and their expressed life satisfactions. All of the respondents are heavily dependent on public resources for their health and well-being, in particular resources such as public housing, health care facilities, and public agencies.

The United States Census Bureau informs us that our aged population continues to grow steadily and, therefore senior citizens will make greater demands on our nation's social delivery system in the future. Many members of this sector of the population belong to ethnic minorities, principally the Black and Hispanic groups. Although differing in cultural heritage, norms, and expectations, both have experienced discriminatory treatment. This becomes an important consideration when policy makers are developing new social programs to serve the urban aged.

The elderly respondents in this study are residents of public housing complexes situated in the New York City area. They are active participants in a pilot demonstration project sponsored by the VERA Institute of Justice. Its main objective is to provide a transportation service designed for the special needs of the aged and physically disabled. Because the 529 persons who responded to the VERA questionnaire were participants in the project, it is possible that they do not constitute a truly representative sample of the inner-city aged, particularly in terms of their anxieties concerning meeting scheduled health and other necessary appointments. We did not anticipate, however, that this type of bias would erase whatever differences might exist otherwise among the three ethnic groups.

The questionnaire developed for the original study inquired into self-care capacities; from whom the respondents received help in a variety of circumstances; interaction with family members, relatives, friends, and agencies; and several aspects of morale and life satisfaction. Of the initial 529 respondents, 424 were persons aged 65 and older, and make up the population under study in this report.

The interest and intent of the research reported here has been to examine the social-support networks of the respondents, their perceived personal health status, and the correlates of life satisfaction as these may vary among the majority and minority ethnic groups represented in the sample. A basic aim was to discover if there were measurable differences among these groups. In addition, the study tried to ascertain if there were any differences in reports of the respondents' social and physical environments; their perceptions of their existing conditions, needs, and services; and the differences that life-long minority status might have on their adjustments to the aging experience.

The majority of respondents in this study were retired and living on retirement income benefits. Most were widowed and had only limited access to resources outside of their immediate neighborhoods.

Our findings serve to refute many of the myths and/or stereotypes regarding the importance of ethnicity for the minority elderly. Although many of the Black and Hispanic elderly had experienced poorer incomes, health, and housing than the White majority during their lives, they tended to receive more assistance from children and kin in times of need. The data indicate that the Hispanic elderly are the most likely to have children with whom they interact frequently and from whom they receive a significant amount of supportive help.

Our elderly Black respondents were almost as likely as the Hispanics to be able to count on support from children and others in time of need. In this regard, other studies emphasize that sheer physical proximity to children is a basic and continuing determinant of the likelihood of receiving help from them. Our data show that the children of White respondents are much more likely to live away from the metropolitan area, and we may assume that such geographical mobility is an opportunity enjoyed more often by members of the majority group. Thus, while minority-group membership serves today as a useful predictor of the relatively high strength of one's informal support network, as discriminatory practices diminish in the future, this "advantage" enjoyed now by Blacks and Hispanics may diminish as well.

In examining the health status of our respondents on the basis of their own reports, we found only limited differences between minority and majority elderly in terms of how they perceive and utilize their health care services. Minority respondents assessed their own health as rather higher than did the majority group respondents, although both groups utilized health care facilities if, when, and as often as necessary.

In exploring our respondents' involvement with three distinct types of formal helping agencies — major governmental agencies, local senior citizen centers, and religious groups — we learned that they make use of them only infrequently. Those respondents who did utilize them, however, did so when they were needed, and with appropriate selectivity.

In general, we can conclude about our respondents that regardless of ethnicity, they are highly satisfied with their housing and neighborhood environments, their physical health, their morale, and their personal autonomy. These findings go hand in hand with the relatively high levels of self-esteem, self-worth, and self-satisfaction they report.

It is meaningful, if not statistically significant, that the minority group respondents expressed higher morale and life satisfaction than their majority group counterparts. An unexpected benefit of membership in a minority group, in other words, lies in the development of informal support networks, for this seems to be of major importance in one's success in adjusting to the experience of aging in urban American Society.

Afterword

After one has lived a life of meaning, death may lose much
of its terror. For what we fear most is not really death but a
meaningless and absurd life. I believe most human beings
can accept the basic fairness of each generation's taking its
turn on the face of the planet if they are not cheated out of
the full measure of their own turn. The tragedy of old age in
America is that we have made absurdity all but inevitable.
We have cheated ourselves. But we still have the possibility
of making life a work of art.

Robert N. Butler
Why Survive: Being Old in America
New York: Harper & Row, 1975, p.422

Appendix

Statistical Procedures

Chapter Six: Life Satisfaction —Morale, Well-Being, and Life Expectations

We were interested in the life satisfaction of the elderly and whether it might be disaggregated into separate dimensions representing trust, optimism, and anxiety. Since most of the data are categorical or nominal, we had to engage in some data transformation by using appropriate procedures to change these variables into a metric.

The procedure that we used was dummy coding (Cohen and Cohen, 1975).[1] The idea of this is that we want the proportion of outcomes of interest for each of the categories of the nominal variables under consideration. For example, the variable of trust had five categories. Each of these in turn would represent a particular level of interest. Therefore by using dummy coding we essentially transformed the data into (pseudo) binomial distributions which have known probabilities, means, proportions, and standard deviations and errors. Such transformed variables are amenable to nonparametric statistical analyses. Basically, nonparametric correlations are for things that are not distributed normally. The coefficients from nonparametric correlation can then be entered into matrix form for use in a principal component factor analysis. This type of factor analysis makes no underlying assumptions about the nature of the data. We could then use the rotated factor solution to provide factor scores as input for the composite scales to be constructed. For each of the three separate sets of factor analyses we developed composite indices of trust, optimism, and anxiety, and the following responses therein. The calculation of these scales are the factor score loadings times the variable minus its mean divided by its standard deviation. In the statistical analyses and computatlon of these factorial scales within the composite indices, we collapsed and combined the scores into high and low rankings. Not all of the scales used in collecting the original data ran the continuum from one extreme to the other. By collapsing the scales into two categories, we were at least able to contrast comparative high versus comparative low for each of the self-responded items.

Notes

[1] Cohen and Cohen, *Applied Multiple REgression Correlation for the Behavioral Sciences.*

Composite Index — Trust

1. Do you feel that most people can or cannot be trusted?

   some of the time   undecided   most of the time

2. Do you feel that most people are helpful or care only for themselves?

   some of the time   undecided   most of the time

3. Do you feel that most people can or cannot be counted on?

   some of the time   undecided   most of the time

4. Do you feel that most people care about you or do you feel alone?

   some of the time   undecided   most of the time

Composite Index — Optimism

1. Would you say that you are . . . ?

   very happy   pretty happy   not very happy

2. Would you say that you worry . . . ?

   quite a lot   sometimes   not at all

3. How do you feel about your housing?

   very satisfied   unsure   very dissatisfied

4. How do you feel about your neighborhood?

   very satisfied   unsure   very dissatisfied

5. How do you feel about your social life?

   very satisfied   unsure   very dissatisfied

6. As you age, are things better, worse, or as you expected?

   better   about the same   worse

Composite Index — Anxiety

1. Do you have control over what happens to you?
   some of the time   undecided   most of the time

2. Do you take things easily or calmly?
   some of the time   undecided   most of the time

3. Would you like more or less to do?
   some of the time   undecided   most of the time

4. Are you able to prepare your own meals?
   without difficulty   some difficulty   needs assistance

5. Are you able to do your own housework?
   without difficulty   some difficulty   needs assistance

6. Are you able to go out-of-doors?
   without difficulty   some difficulty   needs assistance

7. Do you stay at home because it is an imposition on someone to take you?
   often   sometimes   never

8. Do you stay at home for fear of being mugged during the day?
   often   sometimes   never

9. Do you have fears of falling in the street?
   often   sometimes   never

Selected Bibliography

Adams, D. "Correlates of satisfaction among the elderly." *The Gerontologist*. Winter (Part I), 1971: 64–68.

Allen, W. "The search for applicable theories of black family life." *Journal of Marriage and the Family*, February, 1978: 117–129.

Allers, J.O. "Puerto Ricans and health: findings from New York City." Monograph #1. New York: Hispanic Research Center, Fordham University, June, 1978.

Alston, J., and C. Dudley. "Age, occupation, and life satisfaction." *The Gerontologist*. Spring, 1973: 58–61.

American Association of Retired Persons (AARP) and the Administration on Aging (AOA) *1984 Profile of Older Americans.*Washington, D.C.: U.S. Department of Health and Human Services, 1984.

Atchley, R.C. *The Social Forces in Later Life*. 4th ed. Belmont, CA: Wadsworth, 1984.

Barrow, G., and P. Smith. *Aging, the Individual, and Society*. 2nd ed. New York: West Publishing Co., 1979.

Bell, B., ed. *Contemporary Social Gerontology: Significant Developments in the Field of Aging*. Springfield, IL: Charles C. Thomas, Pub., 1976.

Bell, D., *et al. Delivering Services to Elderly Members of Minority Groups: A Critical Review of the Literature.* Santa Monica, CA: The Rand Corporation, 1976.

Bengston, V.E. Olander, and A. Haddad. "The Generation gap and aging family members: Toward a conceptual model." *Roles and Self in Old Age.* Ed. Jaber E.F. Gubrium. New York: Human Sciences Press, 1976: 237–263.

Berghorn, F., *et al. The Urban Elderly: A Study of Life Satisfaction.* Montclair, NJ: Landmark Studies, 1978.

Billingsley, A. "Black families and white social science." *Journal of Social Issues* 26(3), 1970: 127.

Bowlby, J. *The Making and Breaking of Affectional Bonds.* London: Tavistock Publications, 1979.

Brody, E. "Aging." *The Encyclopedia of Social Work.* New York: National Association of Social Workers, 1971: 51.

Bultena, G., and R. Oyler. "Effects of health on disengagement and morale." *Aging and Human Development* 2(2), 1971: 142–148.

Bultena, G.W., and E.A. Powers. "Denial of age identification and reference group orientation." *Journal of Gerontology* 33, 1976: 748–754.

Cantor, M. "The elderly in the inner city: Some implications of the effect of culture on life styles." Paper presented to the Institute on Gerontology and Graduate Education for Social Work, Fordham University, 1973.

_____. "Life space and the social support system of the inner-city elderly of New York." Paper presented at the 26th Annual Meeting of the Gerontological Society, Miami Beach, Florida, 1973.

_____. "Health of the inner city elderly." Paper presented at the 27th Annual Meeting of the Gerontological Society, Portland, Oregon, 1974.

_____. "The informal support system of the familyless elderly — Who takes over?" Paper presented at the 31st Scientific Meeting of the Gerontological Society, Dallas, Texas, 1978.

_____. "Caring for the frail elderly: Impact on family, friends, and neighbors." *Financial Incentives for Informal Caregiving: Proceedings of a Research Utilization Workshop, October 1981.* Ed. Carole A. Snyder (ed.), New York: Research Utilization Project on Aging, Community Council of Greater New York, 1981.

Cicirelli, V. "Adult children's attachment and helping behavior to elderly parents: A path model." *Journal of Marriage and the Family*, 1983: 815–825.

Clark, M. "Patterns of aging among the elderly poor of the inner-city." *The Gerontologist* Spring (Part II), 1971: 58–66.

Clark, M., and B. Anderson. *Culture and Aging.* Springfield, IL: Charles C. Thomas, 1967.

Cockerham, W.C., K. Sharp, and J. Wilcox. "Aging and perceived health status." Journal of Gerontology 38, 1983: 349–355.

Cohen, P., and P. Cohen. *Applied Multiple Regression Correlation for the Behavioral Scientist.* New York: John Wiley & Sons, 1975.

Community Council of Greater New York. *Dependency in the Elderly of New York City: Policy and Service*

Implications of the U.S.-U.K. Cross-National Geriatric Community Study, 1978.

Conklin, J. "Robbery, the elderly, and fear: An urban problem in search of solution." *Crime and the Elderly.* Ed. J. and S. Goldsmith. Lexington, MA: Lexington Books, 1976: 99–110.

Creecy, R., and R. Wright. "Morale and informal activity with friends among black and white elderly." *The Gerontologist* 19(6), 1979: 544–547.

Cumming, E., and W. Henry. *Growing Old: The Process of Disengagement.* New York: Basic Books, 1961.

Cutler, N. "Age variations in the dimensionality of life satisfaction." *Journal of Gerontology* 34(4), 1979: 573–578.

Donnenwerth, G., R. Guy, and M. Norwell. "Life satisfaction among older persons: Rural-urban and racial comparisons." *Social Science Quarterly* 59(3), 1978: 578–583.

Dowd, J., and V. Bengston. "Aging in minority populations: An examination of the double jeopardy hypothesis." *Journal of Gerontology* 33(3), 1978: 427–436.

Drabek, T., and K. Boggs. "Families in disaster: Reactions and relatives." *Journal of Marriage and the Family* 30, 1968: 433–457.

Ehrlich, I.F. "Toward a social profile of the aged black population in the United States: An exploratory study." *The International Journal of Aging and Human Development* 4(3), 1973: 271–275.

Elwell, F., and A. Crannel. "The impact of role loss upon coping resources and life satisfaction of the elderly." *Journal of Gerontology* 36(2), 1981: 223–232.

Estes, C., R. Newcomer, *et al. Fiscal Austerity and Aging. Shifting Government Responsibility for the Elderly.* Beverly Hills, CA: Sage Publications, 1983.

Ferraro, K. F. "Self-ratings of health among the old and old-old." *Journal of Health and Social Behavior* 21, 1980: 377–383.

Fillenbaum. G. G. "Social contexts and self-assessments of health among the elderly." *Journal of Health and Social Behavior* 20, 1979: 45–51.

Gelwicks, L. *Transportation and Its Influence upon the Quality of the Older Person's Relation with the Environment.* Los Angeles, CA: University of Southern California, 1970.

_____. *Planning, Environment and the Older Person.* Washington, D.C.: National Council on the Aging, 1973.

Gibson, G. "Kin Family Network." *Journal of Marriage and the Family* 34, 1972: 13–23.

Gil, F.T. and M. Negm. *Policy Issues Concerning the Hispanic Elderly.* Washington, D.C.: Federal Council on the Aging, Special Aging Populations Committee.

Golden, H. "Life satisfaction among black elderly in the inner city." Paper presented at the 29th Annual Meeting of the Gerontological Society. New York, 1976.

Gottlieb, B. ed. *Social Networks and Social Support.* Sage Studies in Community Mental Health, 4th ed. Beverly Hills, Ca.: Sage Publications, 1981.

Hanrieder, B., J. Williams, and M. Mayer. *The Elderly in New York City, 1970–1980: Selected Demographic Characteristics by Borough.* New York: New York City Department for the Aging, 1981.

Harris, L. *The Myth and Reality of Aging in America.* Washington, D.C.: National Council on the Aging, 1975.

_____. *Aging in the Eighties: America in Transition.* Washington, D.C.: National Council on the Aging, 1981.

Hayes, W., and C. Mindel. "Extended kinship relations in black and white families." *Journal of Marriage and the Family*, 1973: 51–57.

Horowitz, A. "Families who care: A study of natural support systems of the elderly." Paper presented at the 31st Annual Meeting of the Gerontological Society, Dallas, Texas, 1978.

Hudson, G.H. "Some special problems of older Black-Americans." *The Crisis* March, 1976: 88–90.

Jackson, J. "Sex and social class variations in black aged parent-adult child relationships." *Aging and Human Development* 2(2), 1976: 96–107.

King, G.C., and E. H. Hall. "Working with the strengths of black families." *Child Welfare* 61(8), 1982: 536–544.

Kirschner, C. "The aging family in crisis: A problem in living." *The Journal of Contemporary Social Work*, 1979: 209–213.

Klemmack, D., and L. Roff. "Fear of personal aging and subjective well-being in later life." *Journal of Gerontology* 39(6), 1984,: 756–758.

Kutzik, A. "American social provisions for the aged: An historical perspective." *Ethnicity and Aging: Theory, Research and Policy.* Ed. D.E. Gelfand and A.J. Kutzik. New York: Springer, 1979.

Lambing, M. "Social class living patterns of retired Negroes." *Gerontologist* 12(Autumn), 1972: 285–289.

Larson, R. "Thirty years of research on the subjective wellbeing of older Americans." *Journal of Gerontology* 33, 1978: 109–125.

Lawton, M.P., and S. Yaffe. "Victimization and fear of crime in elderly public housing tenants." *Journal of Gerontology* 35(5), 1980: 768–779.

Litwak, E. "Extended kin relations in an industrial society." *Social Structure and the Family.*

Lopata, H. Z. "Widowhood and husband sanctification." *Journal of Marriage and the Family,* 1981: 439–450.

McCaslin, R., and W. R. Calvert. "Social indicators in black and white: Some ethnic considerations in delivery of service to the elderly." *Journal of Gerontology* 30(1), 1975: 60–66.

Maddox, G.L., and E. B. Douglas. "Self assessment of health." *Journal of Health and Social Behavior* 14, 1973: 87–93.

Manuel, R., and M. Berk. "A look at similarities and differences in older minority populations." *Aging* May–June, 1983: 21–29.

Mancini, J. "Family relationships and morale among people 65 years of age and older." *American Orthopsychiatric Association* 49(2), 1979: 292–300.

Merton, R. *Social Theory and Social Structure.* New York:
The Free Press, 1968.

Mindel, C., and C. Vaughan. "A multi-dimensional
approach to religiosity and disengagement." *Journal of
Gerontology* 33(1), 1978: 103–108.

Morrison, B.J. "Physical health and the minority aged."
Aging in Minority Groups. Ed. R. B. McNeely and J.
W. Cohen. Beverly Hills, CA: Sage Publications, 1973:
161–173.

Myles, J.A "Institutionalization and sick role identification
among the elderly." *American Sociological Review*
43(4), 1978: 508–521.

_____. "Needs of the Hispanic Elderly." Select Committee
on Aging, House of Representatives. Ninety-fifth
Congress, Second Session, March, 1978. Committee
Publication No. 95–152. Washington, D.C.: U.S.
Government Printing Office, 1978.

National Urban League Research Department and New York
City Office for the Aging. *The Black Aged in New York
State: A Graphic Analysis.* Prepared for the New York
State Conference on the Black Aged, June 1974.

Palmore, E. "Variables related to needs among the aged
poor." *Journal of Gerontology* 26, 1971: 524–531.

_____. "Compulsory vs. flexible retirement: Issues and
facts." *The Gerontologist* 12(4), 1972: 343–348.

Palmore, E., and F.C. Jeffers. *Predictors of Life Span.*
Lexington, MA: Lexington Books, D.C. Heath &
Company, 1971.

Palmore, E., and C. Luikart. "Health and social factors related to life satisfaction." *Journal of Health and Social Behavior* 13, 1972: 68–80.

Philblad, C., and R. MacNamara. "Social adjustment of elderly people in three small towns." *Older People and Their Social World*. Ed. A. Rose and W. Peterson. Philadelphia: S.A. Davis, Publishers, 1965.

Quarantelli, E.L. "A note on the protective function of families in disasters." *Marriage and Family Living*, 1960: 263–264.

Register, J.C. "Aging and race: A black-white comparative analysis." *The Gerontologist* 21(4), 1981: 438–443.

Riley, M.W. "Social gerontology and age stratification in society." *The Gerontologist* 11, 1971: 79–87.

Rose, A. "Physical health and mental outlook among the aging." *Older People and Their Social World*. Ed. A. Rose. Philadelphia: Davis, 1965.

Rosenmayr, L. "The family: A source of hope for the elderly." *Family, Bureaucracy and the Elderly*. Ed. E. Shanas and M. B. Sussman. Durham, NC: Duke University Press: 132–157.

Rosow, I. *Socialization to Old Age*. Berkeley, CA: University of California Press, 1974.

Sainer, J., and M. Mayer. *Facts for Action*. New York City Department for the Aging #3-1984-A Monograph, 1984.

Sauer, W. "Morale of the urban aged: A regression analysis by race." *Journal of Gerontology* 32(5), 1977: 600–608.

Schwartz, A., C. Snyder, and J. Peterson. *Aging and Life: An Introduction to Gerontology.* 2nd ed. New York: Holt, Rinehart & Winston, 1984.

Schuster, K. ed. "The politics of feeding the elderly." *Journal of Food Management* (March), 1983: 46–79.

Shanas, E. "Family-kin networks and aging in cross-cultural perspective." *Journal of Marriage and the Family* (August), 1973: 505–511.

_____. "The family as a social support in old age." *The Gerontologist* 19(April), 1979: 169–174.

_____. "Older people and their families: The new pioneers." *Journal of Marriage and the Family* (February), 1980: 9–15.

Shanas, E., *et al.* "The psychology of health." *Middle Age and Aging.* Ed. Neugarten. Chicago: University of Chicago Press, 1968.

Siegel, J., and M. Davidson eds. *Demographic and Socioeconomic Aspects of Aging in the United States.* Washington, D.C.: U. S. Department of Commerce, Bureau of the Census, Current Population Reports, 1984.

Silverstein, M., and M. Mayer. "Determinants of health care service utilization among recipients of an urban home-delivered meals program." Paper presented at the 36th Annual Scientific Meeting of the Gerontological Society of America, San Francisco, 1983.

Simmel, A., *et al. The Easy Ride Research Project.* New York: VERA Institute of Justice, 1978.

Simpson, J. "Prisoners of our silver ghettos." *Black Enterprise* (September), 1981: 45–48.

Snyder, Carole ed. *Maximizing Utilization of Community-Based Services by the Minority Elderly: Directions from Recent Research. Proceedings of a Research Utilization Workshop, May 1981.* New York: Community Council of Greater New York, 1981.

Spreitzer, E., and E. Snyder. "Correlates of life satisfaction among the aged." *Journal of Gerontology* 29(4), 1974: 454–458.

Staples, R. "Towards a sociology of the black family: A theoretical and methodological assessment." *Journal of Marriage and the Family* 33, 1971: 119–138.

Streib, G. and C. Schneider. *Retirement in American Society: Impact and Process.* Ithaca, NY: Cornell University Press, 1971.

Sussman, M. "Relationships of adult children with their parents in the United States." *Social Structure and the Family: Generational Relations.* Ed. Ethel Shanas and Gordon F. Streib. Englewood Cliffs, NJ: Prentice-Hall, 1965: 62–92.

Toch, H. "Attitudes of the 'fifty plus' age group: Preliminary considerations toward a longitudinal survey." *Public Opinion Quarterly* 17, 1953: 391–394.

Tissue, T. "Another look at self-rated health among the elderly." *Journal of Gerontology* 27, 1972: 91–94.

Treas, J. "Family support systems for the aged: some social and demographic considerations." *The Gerontologist* 17(December), 1977: 486–491.

Trindad, L., and S. Barg."Facilitating Utilization of Services by Puerto Rican Elderly: A Positive Approach." Office of Aging, Office of Human Development, H.E.W. Region III.

Troll, L., S.J. Miller, and R. C. Atchley. *Families in Later Life*. Belmont, CA: Wadsworth Publishing Co, 1979.

Tull, D., and G. Albaum. *Survey Research: A Decisional Approach*. New York: Intext Educational Publishers, 1973.

United States Department of Commerce, Bureau of the Census. *Projections of the Population of the United States, By Age, Sex, and Race*. 1985: 1983–2000.

United States Department of Housing and Urban Development, Office of Policy Development and Research. *How Well Are We Housed?* vol. 1. *The Hispanics*. Washington, D.C.: United States Government Printing Office, 1978.

Ward, R. "Limitations of the family as a supportive institution in the lives of the aged." *The Family Coordinator* (October), 1978: 365–373.

Watson, W., and R. Maxwell. *Human Aging and Dying: A Study in Socio-Cultural Gerontology*. New York: St. Martin's Press, 1977.

Weeks, J., and J. Cuellar. "The role of family members in the helping networks of older people." *The Gerontologist* 21(4), 1981: 388–394.

White House Mini-Conference on Hispanic Aging. Final Report. Prepared by The National Association for Hispanic Elderly, February, 1981.

Williams, J.A., Jr., and R. Stockton. "Black family structures and functions." *Journal of Marriage and the Family* (February), 1973: 39–49.

Williams, B. 1980 *Characteristics of the Black Elderly. Statistical Reports on Older Americans*. U. S.

Department of Health and Human Services. D.H.E.W. Publication # (OHDS)-80-20057, April 1980.

Wolf, J. *et al.* "Distance and contacts: Interactions of black urban elderly adults with family and friends." *Journal of Gerontology* 38(4), 1983: 465–471.

Index

age distribution, xiv–xv

attachment behavior, 18, 19, 20

Board of Estimate, 68

Brody, Stanley, xviii

Bureau of Census, xiii, 87

Bureau of Purchased Special Services, 67

Catholicism, 67

children, 17, 18, 21, 22, 24–37, 40–41

Church, 62–67

crime, 73–75

disease, xviii

Easyride, xxi, xxii–xxiv, 6, 7, 15

environmental satisfaction, xx–xxii

Family and adult Services, 67

functionality, 23

gender, xv–xvii

gerontology, xxii, 69

government spending, xx

health, xviii–xx; and family, 52; and marital status, 47; expectations, 44; factors, xix; impressions of, xix; impairments, xix; index of, xix;

helping agencies, 55

income, xvi, xx, 12, 13, 14, 15; poverty, 5

Judaism, 67

life expectancy, xiv, xv, 3, 12

life satisfaction, xvii, xx–xxii, 43, 69, 70, 86

marital status, xv, 4

Medicaid, 56, 66, 67

Medicare, 56, 67

migration, xv

neighborhood, xvii–xviii

New York City Dept. for the Aging, 21

New York City Senior
    Center, 68

physicians, 53

population, xiii–xiv, xvi,
    3, 87

primary support system,
    xx

protective behavior, 19

Protestantism, 67

relatives, 38–41

sample group:
    composition, 4; living
    arrangements, 4;
    location, 3

senior centers, 57–62

service utilization, 57

Social Security, 56, 66

social support, 17

statistical analysis, 6, 7, 9,
    93–94

unemployment, 12

VERA, xvii, xxii–xxiv, 4;
    objective of, xxiii, 87

    widows, 10

DATE DUE

MR 17 '95

5/20/99

Demco, Inc. 38-293